TURNING
NEW LIVES
IN INDIA
EAST

TURNING
NEW LIVES
IN INDIA EAST

Twenty Westerners and Their Spiritual Quests

Edited by
MALCOLM TILLIS
and
CYNTHIA GILES

PARAGON HOUSE PUBLISHERS
New York, New York

First edition, 1989
Published in the United States by
Paragon House
90 Fifth Avenue
New York, NY 10011

Copyright © 1989 by Paragon House Publishers

Religion Editor: Don Fehr
Production Editor: Ed Paige
Copy Editor: Rosemary Warden
Designed by Deirdre Amthor

Library of Congress Cataloging-in-Publication Data

Tillis, Malcolm, 1926–
    Turning East : new lives in India : twenty westerners and their
spiritual quests / interviews by Malcolm Tillis ; edited by Cynthia
Giles.—1st ed.
        p.   cm.
    Includes index.
    ISBN 1-55778-228-8
    1. Religious biography—India. 2. Spiritual life. 3. India—
Religion—20th century. 4. Interviews—India. I. Giles, Cynthia.
II. Title.
BL2007.7.T55   1989
294′.092′2—dc20
    [B]   89-33236
                                                         CIP

Manufactured in the United States of America

The paper used in this publication meets the minimum requirements of
American National Standard for Information Sciences—Permanence of Paper
for Printed Library Materials, ANSI Z39.48-1984.

To the memory
of
Sant Darshan Singh
1921–1989
lyric poet
perfect disciple
humble guru

Table of Contents

viii Contents

PART TWO

PART THREE

Author's Preface

During the eleven years I lived in India I was often lent or sent books about Westerners who had also come to India. But they were invariably about those Westerners who had been drawn onto the guru-trail that occasionally leads innocent victims into the hungry jaws of a white-bearded, impressively robed monster who leaves them more spiritually and materially bankrupt than before. These books were very often amusing, sometimes bitter, but nearly always prejudiced or misinformed. They made me wonder why no in-depth study had appeared dealing with the many Westerners who have taken the plunge, left the bright lights of home and are now living fulfilled lives in this vast, fascinating country. There is no shortage of books on India's host of saints, seers and gurus, but what about their Western disciples? Why has so little appeared by them, or about their achievements? They may have taken to the simple life, but surely they are not all under vows of silence.

I felt so strongly about this that I took courage, went out into the field, and collected their experiences myself. This book is the result. It is the outcome of a concentrated five-month journey that took me all over India. Sometimes I traveled under dreadful conditions for days on end in the hope of tracking down someone I had heard about. I traveled alone, reluctantly at first, until after many setbacks I was given much needed strength and reassurance by being thrown head-long into the center of a miracle which is described in the narrative. The result of this experience alone will stay with me for the rest of my life.

My intention from the start was simple enough: to tape record the personal stories of as many followers of different paths, disciplines or gurus as possible. This seemed to me the most accurate way to capture their histories, the reasons why they changed their lives—and most important—what they considered the benefits from having turned East for the new life.

Above all, my intention was to publish their accounts in their own words without superimposing my own views and values. It was not especially important to me how long each person had been in India, although I caught up with some who had arrived over fifty years ago. (Russell Balfour-Clarke's ticket was paid for in 1909 by Mrs. Annie Besant, the President of the Theosophical Society, and thus he was given the remarkable task of teaching English to the thirteen-year-old J. Krishnamurthi.)

This commitment to the new life does not exclude dedicated fol-lowers of the Judeo-Christian tradition: Anil Bhai, born John Davis into an English Catholic family, and still very much a Catholic, is but one example. It was each person's total commitment to a chosen path, and above all why it was being pursued in India, which was the deciding factor for inclusion in the project.

For those attached to a guru or lama whether by vows or initiation, I soon noticed that the truly dedicated disciple reflects at least some of his mentor's consciousness. And that consciousness finds expression through the disciple's life-style, through his manner of speech and actions. It was because of this close, personal attachment that several portraits of a particularly intimate nature, rarely seen in print, were captured describing the unique qualities of some of India's most cel-ebrated saints: the French-born Vijayananda on Anandamay Ma, Maggi

Lidchi on the Aurobindo Mother, the Polish-born Lucia Osborne on Ramana Maharshi.

The printed word often veils the expressiveness and subtle shades of meaning conveyed by the spoken word. In the editing of these interviews I have done my best to retain each person's individual speech rhythms and idiosyncrasies. As English was not always the mother tongue of the person interviewed, this proved yet another challenge. It is, however, a cause of sadness to me that I have been unable to indicate in print the shining quality and vocal expressiveness which were often complimented by radiant facial expressions when the other-worldly beauty of the new life was being described.

Anyone who can reveal to another person his potential for experiencing the Divine within himself is surely to be revered. Most devotees, nevertheless, are inclined to revere their own guru to the exclusion of all others. This often leads to suspicion and to what I call guru-protectiveness, and this sometimes made communication and enquiry from an outsider difficult. It was particularly difficult at the ashrams of Swami Muktananda and Satya Sai Baba; with Muktananda, after twenty-four hours of pleading, placating, I left without even unpacking my tape-recorder (they had actually agreed to the interviews by letter); with Sai Baba I persisted, accepted all sorts of conditions, and came away not only with a double interview but an experience I am not likely to forget.

However, most of those I met were far more approachable and co-operative although in some cases not easy to tie down. In one ashram I was kept waiting five days before the person I wished to interview could give me an hour of her time; but the interview is unique as it vividly illustrates the whole meaning of selfless service, and what it is like to be close to a guru and serve him under conditions of great trust.

I was constantly aware of the contrasts created by the abandonment of the old life for the new. What was the former principal clarinet of the Rotterdam Symphony Orchestra doing wearing flowing red robes? Or the Italian priest editing a Sanskrit magazine? Or the Californian dentist's assistant looking after the hundred-and-four-year-old Sant Gulab Singh? And did the actress from New Zealand have to go all the way to Poona to become a *sannyasi*? I found the dynamic Simonetta, once Italy's foremost woman fashion designer, happy to sleep on the floor of her ashram room. Tensin Palmo, a librarian from London, preferred living in a cave twelve thousand feet above sea level. The Steiners from Australia had settled for a bungalow in the foothills of the Himalayas.

All these dramatic contrasts have helped me to understand that just as there are so many paths leading to fulfillment, so are there travelers on the way. The routes adopted by the people I interviewed are particularly rich: starting off from seventeen different countries in the West they embraced various sects within Hinduism, Buddhism, and Christianity, as well as the Radhasoami Faith, Sikhism, and a synthesis of Hinduism and Christianity as expounded by Father Bede Griffiths.

I encouraged all those who agreed to speak to be frank about the difficulties which are encountered along all paths of endeavor. Some have been remarkably frank. Some spoke only on condition that a transcript would be sent to them before publication. Only in one case did the person interviewed wish to conceal the name of his guru. Four have become gurus themselves, a remarkable attainment in a country not lacking in home talent.

In all I collected fifty-four interviews. It soon became clear that to publish them together in one volume was impractical. It was here that Cynthia Giles with her patience, expertise and sensitivity came to my aid. I must thank her for helping me to choose and edit the selection appearing here. Too many others have been instrumental in encouraging and supporting me to be individually named: they know they have my gratitude.

The many remarkable people I met while working on this project have been a constant source of wonder and inspiration. Some of them have since become close friends. They may have come from diverse backgrounds, they may now be treading diverse paths, yet I see one unifying truth: once people pass through the gate into higher consciousness, no matter what manner of life-style they adopt, no matter where they choose to live, no matter if they eventually return to the West, they can never truly pass back through that gate into the old life.

Many of those I interviewed have adopted Sanskrit or Tibetan names, and a few have become Indian nationals. By turning East, however, all of them are out of Western context climatically, culturally, psychologically. So the question remains: in order to live the new life was it absolutely necessary to make such a dramatic change? Let them speak for themselves.

Malcolm Tillis
Mussoorie, India
Aberdovey, Wales

Editor's Introduction

For most Westerners, India is a mystery—a mixed-up jumble of dreadful poverty and fabulous wealth, sublime religious experience and incredible violence, that challenges our whole understanding of society. India can claim both the world's most populous democracy and the remnants of the world's most rigid system of class distinction; on one level of the Indian value system, life is paramount, while on another, it is trivial. India is intensely spiritual, yet intensely carnal; many of its ashrams celebrate austerity and celibacy, while its palaces offer unparalleled examples of material splendor and its ancient caves contain images of sensuality which transcend the ordinary boundaries of erotic power.

This exotic, kaleidoscopic mystery of India has for a long time both drawn and repelled the Western imagination. India seems extremely foreign to us, and yet somehow familiar, as if our roots are there, as if we recognize still existing in India a way of being which was once the common experience of humanity. The anachronisms, the contra-dictions, the extremes that exist in India generate a tremendous mag-netic tension which simultaneously fascinates and frightens those of us who live in a more consistent and comfortable world.

I, for one, would be frightened at the idea of living in India. But at the same time, I have to struggle against feeling that somehow I *ought* to, that there are certain transformations, transcendences that can only take place there. In actual fact, I don't believe that's true; as many people say in this book, spiritual progress is possible any-where if the soul is willing. Still, India seems the repository of potent energies and special wisdom, accumulated and intensified for cen-turies. India beckons the seeker.

It is not merely the content of Indian culture which beckons (and baffles) the spiritual aspirant; it is the very style of understanding the world, a style which is quite different in India than anywhere else. One of the most salient points of this difference is what I think of as "serene irony." I first glimpsed this characteristic of the Indian point of view when I read one of the best-known parts of the Rig Veda, a segment often referred to as the "creation hymn." At first I thought the tone must be an imposition of the translator, a form of poetic license. But since then I have read many different translations of these lines, and all, in their different ways, reveal the same quality of consciousness underlying the words of the Rig Veda. I choose this translation (by R.T.H. Griffith, 1889) because it is a classic, and con-veniently at hand:

> Then was not non-existent nor existent: there was no realm of air, no sky beyond it.
> What covered it, and where? and what gave shelter? Was water there, unfathomed depth of water?
> Death was not then, nor was there aught immortal: no sign was there, the day's and night's divider.
> That One Thing, breathless, breathed by its own nature: apart from it was nothing whatsoever.
> Darkness there was: at first concealed in darkness this All was indiscriminated chaos.
> All that existed then was void and formless: by the great power of Warmth was born that Unit.

Thereafter rose Desire in the beginning, Desire, the primal seed and germ of Spirit.

Sages who searched with their heart's thought discovered the existent kinship in the non-existent.

Transversely was their severing line extended: what was above it then, and what below it?

There were begetters, there were mighty forces, free action here and energy up yonder.

Who verily knows and who can here declare it, whence it was born and whence comes this creation?

The Gods are later than this world's production. Who knows then whence it first came into being?

He, the first origin of this creation, whether he formed it all or did not form it, whose eye controls this world in highest heaven, he verily knows it, or perhaps he knows not.

What made this passage so fascinating to me was that it seemed to attack quite directly the central problem of understanding existence, which is the problem of grasping its relationship to *non*existence. The kind of cheerful-yet-vulnerable "wondering" which goes on in the passage above was unique in my own experience, as my education had been centered around the study of Western philosophy. By comparison with the Rig Veda, I thought, even Socrates seemed a bit whiney and dogmatic about the universe, and everyone else, from Aquinas to Sartre, appeared downright childish.

The Rig Veda, apparently the earliest of the Indian sacred texts, abounds with curiosity about the world, and with a calm willingness to accept ambiguity and uncertainty. This initially amazed me—and here my own naiveté of those days is patent—because that attitude seemed such a sophisticated one for so long ago. (The dating of the Rig Veda is uncertain, but the weight of scholarly opinion tends to support a date between 1500 and 900 B.C.; there are other sacred texts—Babylonian and Egyptian, for example—which are probably older, but then they are not part of a living spiritual tradition today.) As I later learned, India has certainly had its own dogmatisms in the interim since the Rig Veda, yet it is still true that something of the Veda's original ironic spirit seems to remain at the center of the Indian experience.

That spirit will be apparent in many of the people you'll meet in the interviews which make up this book. Melita Maschman's story is a good example. She relates in her interview the first meeting she had with the great Indian saint Anandamayi Ma. Maschman, who found herself "accidentally" with the opportunity for a meeting with Ma, composed a list of important philosophic questions she wished to ask the revered woman. Ma, reclining on her divan, listened with relish to the first questions, then broke out laughing, and continued to laugh uproariously until Maschman withdrew in fury. For many years after that, whenever she encountered Maschman—who became a devotee and lived near the ashram—Ma would burst into laughter all over again.

What on earth is the Westerner to make of such behavior? This kind of cosmic hilarity is not uncommon in the spiritual circles of India, though at other times the utmost seriousness may prevail. Ma, for example, was extremely orthodox, not to say rigid, in most of the requirements she placed on disciples. A strict caste system prevailed in her ashrams, and dietary laws were enforced absolutely. Yet those around her reported a joy and freedom felt in her presence which surpassed anything else they had known.

Again, contrasts and contradictions—and the ironic acceptance of whatever *is*; that is the way of India. Without going there and living, it is very difficult to grasp the essential difference which distinguishes the Indian ethos from our own. And that is why those of us not planning to relocate our lives to India have reason to be grateful to Malcolm Tillis, who has captured in this remarkable book of interviews the flavor, texture, and import of spiritual life in India, as seen through the eyes of Westerners who have chosen to live there. Through their candid reflections, it is possible for the rest of us to get "inside" the Indian experience in a way that hasn't been possible before.

Each of the stories recounted here is different—some are wildly different!—yet there are common threads which run throughout them all. Perhaps the most important of these common threads is the intense desire felt by all the people here to focus their lives on the activity of spiritual development. Some recognized this need early in life, while others were unaware of it even when they went to India. But all report a feeling of incompleteness in their Western lives, and a momentum which seemed to carry them, wittingly or not, to the shores of India.

Many of the interviewees are people who went to India long before the Beatles made it fashionable; others are people young enough to have been among the Beatles' teenage fans. Through their various stories, we as readers perceive the spiritual currents which eddy throughout the world, bearing certain souls one way, certain souls another. Not one person who speaks here feels that he or she consciously chose or controlled the particular path which they ultimately came to follow. Rather the paths, it seems, chose them. But that was only possible, all agree, because they were willing to open themselves to the possibilities.

Some of the people in this book left marriages and children for spiritual "exile" in India; some left thriving careers, notoriety, and wealth. Others cast themselves loose from parents, from security, from futures they could imagine, choosing instead an unforeseeable journey toward an unknowable destination. They literally traded old lives for new ones, and not for any reason which is commonly recognized as sensible in the West. Many of the characteristics of life in India are in fact exactly the ones which most Westerners are trying to escape *from*, not move toward; these characteristics often—though not always—include hard beds (or none at all), stifling heat, tiresome food, voracious insects, bitter cold, dull labor, and rigid routine.

One of the fascinations of reading these interviews is coming to understand *why they did it*, why all these people chose to seek new lives that entailed significant hardships and offered no conventional rewards. The reasons become clear in the course of the book, for although we hear a good deal about the trials of ashram life, we also hear about the triumphs of the spirit which make it all worthwhile. These triumphs are not as a rule of the flashy sort—no instantaneous illuminations, no miraculous seizures, just patient work and, little by little, a sense of growth, discovery, fulfillment. The stories here are earnestly human ones, stories with which the rest of us can identify and from which we can learn.

Malcolm Tillis, who trekked around India for months gathering these interviews, has described them as "human adventure stories," and that is very apt. There is adventure here, high drama, but it unfolds in the realm of consciousness rather than in lost diamond mines or hidden lagoons. And because the stories are told so unselfconsciously and candidly, in response to Malcolm's gentle presence, they are accessible—and absorbing. From them we can learn not only what it is like to live in the spiritual world of India, but also something about the nature of the spiritual life itself, wherever it may be lived.

Perhaps the most splendid thing about this book, from my own point of view at least, is the fact that I have learned from it more about Indian thinking and about spiritual discipline than I have from the laboriously "informational" books on these topics which I have forced myself to read. Gradually, as one reads these interviews, an understanding grows—the sort of understanding which is difficult to achieve when reading "about" something, and yet is almost effortlessly accomplished by talking *with* a person who speaks from experience. One has the sense of being part of a long, rich discussion, from which all manner of new ideas and deepened perceptions may arise.

You will not like everyone you meet in this book, I imagine, though you will probably love some of them and remember them all your life. There are saintly people here, and there are "reformed" rogues. There are exceptionally brave people (like the young English woman who lives alone in a Himalayan cave, or the former fashion designer who works with lepers), and there are unusually imaginative ones (like the couple who are raising their four children in an encampment of exiled Tibetan Buddhists). Many religious persuasions are represented here, and many attitudes toward spiritual life.

What is *not* much encountered in this book, on the other hand, is pretentiousness or preaching—or perfection. By no means are the interviewees here fully realized, nor do they claim to be. You will see the whole spectrum of human nature, from pettiness to magnanimity, egotism to selflessness, cynicism to ecstasy, revealed in the words of these interviews. You will also sense in each person's dialogue an earnest desire to move ever toward the good. In addition, then, to being a book about India and the spiritual life, it is a book about people, and there is no richer, more important subject.

One of the people this book is also "about" is Malcolm Tillis himself. In the 1950s, Malcolm was a musician with the Halle Orchestra, under the direction of Sir John Barbirolli. After writing a successful book about orchestra life, Malcolm went to Ibiza, where he lived a very attractive life as a designer and boutique owner. But at the age of forty, Malcolm suddenly decided to seek a quieter, more contemplative life on the island of Malta. Here, with his wife (novelist Kate Christie), he began a spiritual search which led eventually to a life in India, where they lived for eleven years. After the death of their guru, they continued their literary work until 1984 when they moved to Wales, where they now live.

In 1980, a project which Malcolm had been contemplating (somewhat reluctantly) for several years finally forced itself upon him. He felt that the many fascinating and inspirational stories around him—stories of Westerners who had come to India on spiritual quests and remained there to lead "new" lives—should be recorded and published; yet he was reluctant to leave his home to face the many difficulties such a project would entail, not the least of which was the demanding, but necessary, travel. Finally he decided that the importance of the task outweighed his own reluctance, especially since many of the people he hoped to interview were very old, and would soon be taking with them into yet another life the rich treasury of experiences they had known in this one.

I feel personally grateful to Malcolm for undertaking this "mission," and I think many readers will share my gratitude. *Turning East* contains interviews with 95-year-old Russell Balfour-Clarke, who recounts with great frankness (and sweetness) his long association with Krishnamurthi and the Theosophical Society, and with 76-year-old Lucia Osborne, widow of Arthur Osborne, who shares her exquisite memories of Ramana Maharshi. These interviews offer unique, personal perspectives on a time early in this century when only a very few Westerners penetrated the veils of Indian spirituality, a time when something began which continues to flower today.

The interviews take us three-quarters of the way through the century, and from one end of India to another. We visit the spare, almost austere ashram of Benedictine monk Father Bede Griffiths, who is creating a synthesis of Christian and Eastern teachings; a lavish Hare Krishna temple, with attached deluxe hotel; a serene and joy-filled home in Chandigarh, where an American follower cares for the 104-year-old guru Sant Gulab Singh; a great gathering of Buddhists who have come to receive the ancient, mystical Lam Dre teachings; and half a dozen other memorable places where Western seekers agreed to share their experiences and insights.

Malcolm has not just gathered and transcribed the interviews in this book; he has woven them together with a tale of his own—the story of his journey among the ashrams of India, uncertain but willing, tape recorder and camera at hand (well, usually). Through Malcolm's narrative, we see the book itself grow and take shape, and we see the changes which take place in Malcolm himself as he encounters perhaps the broadest cross-section of spiritual seekers that anyone has yet explored. It is through Malcolm's generous willingness to open himself to all these experiences that we, as readers, become privileged to look inside a small, scattered and unusually interesting human community—a community of people who have uprooted and transplanted themselves for the sake of spiritual flowering.

Cynthia Giles

Part One

Anandamayi Ma is India's most widely known woman saint. Her name means "The Bliss-Intoxicated Mother," although she has been bliss-intoxicated since childhood. Her physical beauty in itself has been extraordinary, and although she is now in her middle eighties, much of that beauty remains. Her spiritual magnetism is unchanged.

She now rarely sings her bhajans, nor discourses, and hardly ever talks to her followers. It is enough for them to sit silently in her physical presence and enjoy her darshan. She has never been abroad, but still travels continually all over India, visiting her many ashrams.

The day I arrive in her Kankhal Ashram in Hardwar, the arrangements for the two interviews that follow, arrangements which had been made for some time, are eclipsed by Ma's sudden decision to give a four-hour darshan—something she has not done for years. All of her devotees are, of course, going to sit before her and absorb; no one is going to leave Ma to come and talk to me. So I, also, sit and absorb; there is nothing else for me to do.

Perhaps I absorb too much, because after Ma retires to her room and we are free to disperse, there is no longer the slightest desire left in me to tape the interviews. In fact, there's a sort of repulsion with my whole plan to go from ashram to ashram, asking questions.

After all, I say to myself, how can you expect devotees to translate into words the kind of experience I've just had? And how am I to ask questions—you can't absorb all this charged radiation and then start asking unnecessary questions. With a flash of relief, I realize that after all this is only the first day, and I can abandon the whole thing. Tomorrow, home!

But suddenly here is Kalidas, who is one of the few foreign disciples—he is American—allowed to live in this ashram. He is excited; he says he has persuaded Vijayananda to give his interview right away. Triumph met by bewilderment; I am still suffering from resented intoxication. Kalidas is already unpacking my tape recorder. "Vijayananda is waiting," Kalidas tells me. There is another flash— a happy one—I can leave early in the morning!

But now we are being introduced, and I see Vijayananda is a gentle, elderly Frenchman who speaks softly, confidentially, and everything he says is punctuated by much quiet laughter. Even when you've absorbed too much and want to escape, you have to respond.

K alidas has been kind enough to tell me you want to know about my background; . . . well, . . . you see, there are two people: one who died on 2 February 1951, the other who was born on 2 February 1951. Now do you want to hear about the dead man or the living man?

Could we try the dead man first?

The dead man has no great interest—he happened to be a doctor interested in spirituality. He already had one guru in France where he had been born, and had practiced meditation for sixteen years before coming to India. You see, from the age of ten he was rather religious—he was a Jew by birth—so this boy, instead of playing like other children, was thinking: What is the nature of God? And it was a big problem, and it lasted many years. Finally he decided that God not being material, the mind or spirit did not exist. So he became an atheist.

This lasted until he was seventeen. He was being trained as a rabbi. He had eaten, *devoured* all Western philosophers but came to the conclusion that religion was a humbug. He was only enthusiastic about Nietzsche. Now what Nietzsche says is a nonsense, but as a teenager the nonsense he didn't catch—what he caught was the spirit. Nietzsche is a mystic. Up till then this boy didn't know what real mysticism was, as he was surrounded by bigoted people. You must know them; they have no religious feeling. I was fully disgusted. But Nietzsche attracted me just for the mystic flame. Later I found the same flame in the *Upanishads* without the nonsense, so I became fully Upanishadic. I stick to Vedanta right up to now, although my first guru was a Buddhist and wanted to make a Buddhist out of me.

So that was the dead man's lovely background. That doctor, who practiced in the south of France and whose guru didn't satisfy him, decided to come to India in 1950.

Thirty years ago it wasn't so popular to come to the East just for spirituality. Did you have to come by boat in those days?

Yes, it was a rarity; very few came for that in those days. The boat landed in Colombo on 1 January 1951—the first day of the second half of the century. I actually arrived in India on the fifteenth. I really came to see Ramana Maharshi; I had not even *heard* of Anandamayi Ma then. But while I was preparing for my trip, he died. Then I thought: I will go and see Aurobindo! But this fellow also ran away to Nirvana a few days before I took the boat. As I had arranged everything, I said, "Well, what is the use?—let me go!"

In Ceylon I stayed in a Buddhist monastery with a German monk: we weren't enthusiastic about each other. He was very dry. Then I went to Pondicherry, to the Aurobindo Ashram, and saw the Mother. Frankly, I didn't feel anything. But as it happened, one Canadian lady who had just come from Benares said, "If you go there [Benares] I will give you something to see—the University, the temples, and Anandamayi's ashram." I asked, "Who is Anandamayi?" She said, "Oh, she is a lady saint." I asked, "She must be old?" "No, no, she is fairly young." Then I asked (I didn't know anything), "But there must only be women with her?" She replied, "There are more men with her than women." So I thought: All right—let me go! But in my imagination I couldn't help thinking she must be some old hump-back. I wanted to go to Rishikesh to see Sivananda, so why not go on and see this lady saint also?

I reached Benares on 1 February 1951 with a letter of introduction to the best man at Ma's ashram. In Benares I had a strange impression that I had come home—a strange impression I would never like to leave. Actually, I knew I had to leave in three weeks—my return passage was booked. Anyway, I went straight to the fellow with my letter. He was not there. I found his nephew, an amazingly handsome boy, and he was the presiding deity who brought me to Ma.

It was nearing sunset. I didn't intend to see her—I just thought I would see the ashram, then go away. But as I entered, Ma came out. She looked at me with a strange look—she doesn't have that look now, slightly up and far away as if she were looking at your destiny, embracing your whole destiny.

Now what struck me first was that she was not a humpback, nor was she old, but handsome, although her great beauty did not strike me at that first moment. Her hair was long and flowing, and it sur-prised me. Could a lady saint be that way? I always thought lady saints must be old, with odd dress. She was all in white. Her simplicity was a shock. Anyhow, I said: Let me stay on—let me see what will happen!

I did not ask for it, but later Ma gave me a private interview. Atmananda* was to interpret. Actually, I had nothing to ask. With a saint you don't ask questions—you want the spiritual contact. But Ma started asking *me* questions—questions very much to the point. At one stage she said that the German professor who had visited her the day before was a worldly man, but that she could see I was marked as a worshiper of *Aum*. That was the first day. I was supposed to go back to my hotel for dinner. But there was a *kirtan*, and this devotional music was like hearing something from a previous life, a sound I yearned to hear again although I had never heard it before. I was filled with joy just listening to this music and singing.

When I got back to my hotel there was a revolution going on inside me—a real revolution. I was overflowing with happiness, with love. It was something extraordinary. I felt I could not leave Ma. You cannot imagine it. Next day I came back to the ashram and asked Ma per-

*Atmananda is one of Ma's oldest western disciples.

mission to stay. I moved out of the hotel and spent that first night nearly thirty years ago without blankets on the ashram floor (there was no bedding). But I was happy. And since that day I have never left Ma.

What happened to your booked passage?
I just canceled everything.

You never left India?
I never left. As I used to be a rather cautious type, I asked for a berth on the next boat. I thought: This may turn out to be a passing fancy. But the next boat left, and the next, and I never used the ticket. I am still here.

When did Ma give you the orange robes?
First I wore my own Western dress. I didn't want to put on white, as it gets dirty quickly and I didn't want to have to keep washing it every day. Then I started wearing white—not a *dhoti* but pajamas. I have a photo taken with Miguel Serrano;* I look like Charlie Chaplin. In those days I neglected my appearance. The main reason was that I didn't want to attract women. When you have this inner awakening, you get a strong attraction power. So for many years I went rather unkempt, even dirty, so as not to attract women.

Now I should explain that Ma doesn't want to give *sannyas* to Westerners; she doesn't want to give them orange robes. At least that's what she says. Now once we were at the Ardha Kumba Mela at Allahabad in 1971. It was the twentieth anniversary of my meeting with Ma. She had been wearing this shawl I now have on—it was white then. She gave it to me saying it could be dyed the color I was then wearing—a brownish yellow. I didn't want to do that; in a kind of joke I said, "But *gerua* [an ocher-red color obtained from natural dyes] would be better." She replied rather sternly, "*Gerua*, no!— you can wear *yogya* [a bright orange obtained only from chemical dyes]." Then turning to someone she told him to dye the shawl for me. I would have been happy with it staying white, but when we were back in Benares, this person came for the shawl, made it orange, and after ten years it is still the same color although it has been washed many times. It wasn't until Ma's eightieth birthday a few

_____
*Miguel Serrano writes about his meeting with Vijayananda in his book *The Serpent of Paradise*.

years ago that she gave me these clothes that are all orange. I would
never have worn them on my own.

Do you ever practice as a doctor these days?
Very rarely. There's an Indian doctor here.

*Although I can see your way of life is so Indian, do you ever think
about going back to the West?*
Yes, frequently—but my link here is Ma. As long as she is in the
body, I don't think I will ever go back.

Can you tell me something about your daily life?
Most of the day I spend in meditation—that's my job. Just as
someone spends seven or eight hours each day in an office, that's my
work. The rest of the time is spent looking after the body, that's all.

*Over the years you must have seen many Westerners in India looking
for spiritual upliftment. Some fall into the hands of imperfect teachers. Can you give any guidelines on how this can be avoided?*
It is very simple. The best way is to have a sincere yearning for
God. You don't have to run after gurus. You need a pure mind and
this yearning, and everything will be arranged by itself. The guru is
not a human being: the guru is all-pervading. So if you want God in
human form, He will send you the guru—His human form. The guru
is more eager to find you than you are to find him. You are just to
open yourself, to purify yourself, to be sincere, not to look for
power—no yearning for power. Then the guru will appear from inside. Those who don't find the guru are not ripe, that's all.

*Since you have been with Ma, have you met any other enlight-
ened teachers?*
Two are very high in my mind. Swami Ramdas, who has passed
away, and Krishnamurthi. Then there is Mother Krishnabai, who is
also very high. I had a short meeting with Neem Karoli Baba. He
impressed me very much; he was so kind to me. I have written about
all this and some of the ashrams I have visited in my little book, *In
the Steps of the Yogis.*

Can you give a description of life in this ashram?
The beauty of Ma's ashram is unlike any other. We are free to do
what we like. There is nothing compulsory—I mean free as far as the
routine goes, not as to behavior. It is unlike other places where you

have to get up at the gong and sit together at fixed times for meals; there's nothing like that here.

But I was under the impression that there are all sorts of rules about the castes not mixing with the Westerners.

That's different. The rules of behavior are extremely severe, that I must say. For example, the rule of *brahmacharya*: everyone is expected to keep perfect chastity; it is the main rule in Ma's ashrams. Then the food: it is the same—very severe. One must eat pure food. That means not only meat is prohibited, but onions and garlic. It is enough to get kicked out if one takes even an *egg* in one's room.

Is there any significance in taking a new name?

I didn't take a new name; it has been given to me by Ma. The significance is that when you come to the feet of the guru, you are born again. It is a second birth. If Ma does something, it has a deep meaning. Ma gave me my name in Anand Kashi, a wonderful place ten miles from Rishikesh in the midst of jungle with a few houses built by the Raj Mata of Tehri Garhwal. She received Ma there in April of 1951, just a few weeks after I had come to her. Ma gave three names at that time: she called the place Anand Kashi, the Raj Mata she called Ananda Priya, and she called me Vijayananda.

What is the translation of your name?

Jaya is victory; *vi* is the superlative; *ananda*, you must know, means bliss. Whatever Ma does has a deep meaning—she is a Divine Being.

But if her devotees ask for a new name, will she not give one?

I will give an example to show she does not. There was an American girl wanting Ma to give her a name ending in *anada*—bliss. Ma looked at me and said, "You give her a name!" Now the strange thing is— to show how Ma works—I could give thousands of names, but my mind became blank like an idiot. Nothing came up—really. Suddenly in this awful blank one name came up: Mirabai—nothing else. It came out by itself. . . . I couldn't *say* anything else! Ma didn't want to give the girl a name herself, but still she was given the name of Mirabai. Ma didn't want a name ending in *ananda*—perhaps the girl didn't deserve it. Most important was that Ma didn't want to refuse her, in case the girl went away feeling she had been rejected. It appeared that I had found the name, but actually Ma had.

Can you give any other examples of how Ma relates to and teaches her Western followers?

If you take Ma as a physical body you see only a tiny part. You must see her as a physical body, but also as being the center of an all-pervading power. What that physical body does and what we see is only a small part of what she does. Sometimes she may be a little distant with Westerners, that I agree. But why do they come? Why do they sit with her so long? They feel bliss inside. Although she may look distant outside, inside she gives them happiness. She may have to make a severe face—perhaps because of those around her who don't like so many Westerners coming. But if she is full of love, what is more real?

What is more real? Why should Ma be influenced by some of her close Indian devotees? Can't they be influenced by what she wants?

It is rather complicated. She herself doesn't want too many Westerners. She has noticed—she has the insight—that Western civilization is totally different from Indian civilization. And not only the civilization, but the spiritual way of life. Here sexual purity is so important, whereas for Westerners it's a trifle. If Indians talk too much to Westerners they automatically become contaminated.

Are all Ma's Indian followers so innocent, so pure?

Yes, I think they are—most observe chastity. You must take into account that when we talk to anyone there's an exchange of vibrations, unwillingly perhaps, but it is there. Indian girls are not allowed to talk to householders or Westerners. There is little contact. When you and I talk together, there is an exchange of minds: you will take something from me; I will take something from you. If you have strong control of mind you will not be influenced by me. But people who don't have this control will be influenced without their knowledge.

Surely Indian renunciates would not be influenced.

Most of them are children, . . . they are *sadhus* in name.

But aren't they given more honor and respect than the Westerners —who I notice have more humility and perhaps greater sincerity? I haven't seen too much humility in Indian sadhus wearing ocher robes. Forgive me for saying this. They are of course fortunate, having been born into high castes—but have they overcome pride and ego?

Part of Ma's spiritual attainment, part of her greatness is that she has come with a special mission. Now this is my personal opinion; it may or may not be true: it is to establish a stronghold of Hindu orthodoxy. Perhaps it's needed, and when anything is needed some divine power puts it there.

But was it so strict when Ma started her mission?

If you examine the background it's easier to understand. When she started—say sixty years ago—she was surrounded by many educated Hindus who admired the West and Western education. The problem was to bring them back to their Hindu culture and show them that their traditions, especially their religious traditions, are higher than the Western ones they admired. It was justified. They were being kicked by the British while continuing to admire them. I know quite a lot of them, although they are now elderly. Ma had to show them: You are Brahmins, therefore superior men; you need not worship foreigners. She wanted to give them pride in their own religion, in their nationality, in their higher caste—instead of crawling before the British. This was the atmosphere in India when Ma started.

Even the Brahmins employed by the British were all for the British; they were servile, despising their own religion. The British ridiculed India and Hinduism, and—to imitate the British—they also scorned their own traditions. That was the background in which Ma started; she has continued that way. I can tell you very plainly that although I have been here so many years—it's almost thirty—I have been put at a disadvantage sometimes. I understand her; she still wants to show them they are not to bow before foreigners: they have a higher civilization; they have a higher religion.

You have been so patient with me, I would like to thank you for explaining all that to me.

You know, in the early days when I arrived here many people asked me why I had decided to leave everything behind—family, friends, country, profession, wealth—to follow Ma. It is always difficult to reply to such questions, not because language lacks words but because a word may not have the same meaning for everyone unless they too have experienced the sensation corresponding to that word. I have clung to Ma like a shadow all these years, sometimes suffering torments whenever I am unable to see her. In those early days I couldn't even understand what she was saying, but I would spend hours at her feet without taking my eyes off her.

You see, from the beginning I had the conviction that I was looking at the Lord Himself incarnated in the body of a woman.

．　．　．

As there are no facilities for visitors to stay in any of Ma's ashrams, I have taken a room in a nearby dharmsala. It was empty except for a string bed. Someone gave me a brush of twigs and a candle. Uma, who is an American (I used to know her before she met Kalidas), gave me her mattress; she has just started her period so she cannot use it. Everything she touches during these three days has to be washed, so of course it's easier to sleep on a string bed than to have to wash her new mattress. Ma is so super-orthodox that Uma will not be able even to enter the ashram until clear of the "infection."

After the Vijayananda interview, Uma gave me a late-night mint tea, which may have helped cancel my plan for an early morning escape and the abandoning of further work on this book. The morning's pale sun is filling me with resignation; there is nothing to do but absorb what there is to be absorbed and swing along.

I am swinging into the next interview (Kalidas has again put in a good word for me) with such renewed spirits that at the end of a breathtaking forty-five-minute saga, I turn over the cassette only to find nothing has been recorded. Another sign: brother, go home! Atmananda is saying coyly, "I told you I didn't want to talk into that machine."

But Atmananda is not heartless. She points across the courtyard, saying, "Look, there's Melita—she's a bit difficult, but once you get her to talk it will be fascination."

I run, but Melita won't speak. She is in a bad mood. She is also a writer, and writers don't always feel like giving away gems they can use themselves. She gives me a published piece she says I can use. . . . "No, you can't take it with you; copy it, dear, copy it!"

I am really, definitely—and right now—about to take the bus back to my home in Mussoorie, but Melita is snatching back the papers, saying, "All right, you be here at 1:15—my bad mood, it may be better then." Melita is German, so who can tell?

So there's time for lunch with Kalidas and Uma, and like sweet and true devotees, they are telling me all about Ma and stretching it out, and I am ten minutes late. And Melita is in a worse mood. She has written me a note saying: Too late. She is pinning it to her dharmsala *door, but the sight of a hopeless, breathless interviewer (*dharmsala *stairs are steep and many) makes her burst into laughter—the mood, it changes. We start.*

MELITA MASCHMAN
a dharmsala Kankhal
Hardwar
29 November 1980

First—I never came to India looking for gurus. Ma I met accidentally. "How?" you will ask. Then it is for you to listen. I was working in Afghanistan as a journalist. Journalists have holidays, so I wanted to spend three weeks with a German family in Mussoorie—that's where you live, right?

Right.

We started from Kabul—all fine—but by the time we reached the nice Himalayan foothills, the rains washed away the road. That meant their fat Mercedes couldn't move. I got out, took my bundle and went to Dehra Dun, making myself independent. After passing a boring hour there, I asked somebody what would be interesting to see. He said, "Take this bus standing at the corner; it goes to Hardwar—that's a lovely place of pilgrimage." I looked round Hardwar . . . not so interesting! So I asked someone else on the street, "Is there something *really* nice to see?" "Much, much," I was told, "take a rickshaw to Kankhal: it has an old Shiva temple, and today a fair is going on."

O.K. Right. Fine. There I found a children's picture-book temple. It is near Ma's ashram. I remember this was my first impression of Indian poverty. The fair was going on, but there were hundreds of beggars sitting along the lanes, among them many lepers. A little time before, I had changed a hundred-rupee note into a clean bundle of one-rupee notes; I started distributing them. This caused five thousand beggars to jump at me. I felt as if my last minute had come— oo-ha! Later someone told me that in the same place two years before, a Rani had been mobbed to death by these violent people.

With their half-eaten faces and hands they were pulling at my bag; they spat in my face. It was shocking. But suddenly two ladies from south India jumped into the crowd, and with great energy howled and pushed and beat these people. They saved me and my handbag—I suppose the poor things thought there must be millions in it. The ladies scolded me terribly—yes, quite terribly—not to give any money; otherwise they run after you.

Anyway, they had saved me. Then, as they had just come to Hardwar, we stayed in a nearby hotel together. We had a nice talk—not too long—when they jumped up saying, "We have to quickly go to our ashram to see our guruji. Wait for us; we shall be back in an hour." They pointed to the ashram; in those days it was the nucleus of today's ashram. I had never even heard of an ashram or a guruji: I thought maybe it was a dentist or something like that.

You live in India, so you will know that whenever anyone says wait for me one hour it means between one and four hours; it does not mean sixty minutes. After waiting one hour and ten minutes I became worried, so I went to the door through which my lovely ladies had vanished. I knocked hard till an unfriendly young man came out and chased me away by banging the door against my nose. After another twenty minutes I knocked again—I thought perhaps they were in trouble; they were so late. This time one of my ladies saw me and made them let me in. Now that I was inside, I could see everyone was quite content to wait a few more hours, but at least I had found out they were not waiting for the dentist, but their common spiritual teacher. I was much relieved.

One very old lady then came out and offered me a glass of water. Someone told me she was the mother of the guruji, Didi Ma. By myself I would not have been able to make out if it was a man or a woman so old was she with a shaven head, *sannyasi* clothes and toothless smile—a sweet smile. Eventually we were allowed to go up to the roof, where we again prepared ourselves for more lovely waiting. We were about twenty-five people.

Then suddenly Ma came out and went up and down, up and down. It was my first intensive impression of this type of people I had ever had—they were a category of entities I had not met before. They started bowing down—*pranaming*—ecstatic, and Ma chatted with them, laughed with them. Someone forced me to put a question—I had no desire to ask anything—but somehow something came out. The reply was translated by one of the *sadhus*. It was in such a nice Indian-English that even one syllable I did not understand. To this day I do not know what Ma said to me at that first meeting.

What I did know was that I was absolutely fascinated by what I saw, although I had no idea of its significance. I am from a Protestant background, and that anyone saintly could be moving amongst us in a physical body seemed to me quite out of the question.

When we got back to the hotel, the two ladies asked if I had an alarm clock. They explained they had to go back to the ashram so they must be up by 4 A.M. I laughed and said, "I will be your alarm clock, because I hardly sleep." The fact is that for years in spite of taking heavy drugs I was unable to sleep soundly.* That night after seeing Ma was a great turning point for me in many ways, and one of them was that the annoyed ladies had to wake *me* at six. Since then I have never had to take anything to encourage sleep.

Now I had nearly three weeks before I had to go back to Kabul, so I decided to circulate around this saintly phenomenon and study it. I was told to carry out the process at Ma's ashram in Rajpur Road near Dehra Dun, where she was to arrive in three days time. There I would be able to look at her more closely, for they said fewer crowds

---

*In her book *Account Rendered* (Abelard-Schuman, 1964), Melita Maschman describes, in the form of a letter to a Jewish school-friend, her work as a leader in the Hitler Youth Movement both before and during the War. At that time, the National Socialist Movement aroused in her and many other young Germans a dedication which induced them to turn a blind eye to the appalling suffering and wholesale massacre of Jews. Nor did she see that Hitler was motivated solely by the lust for power. For this abnegation of her conscience and her will she paid after the War by a three-year jail sentence and an almost unbearable weight of disillusion and remorse. The damage done to her, and her inability to come to terms with it, were partly healed when a Jewish woman met her with a spontaneous gesture of friendship.

come. By then, Atmananda, who is Ma's oldest Western devotee, had given me some information and said, "You ask Ma questions and see how wonderful the answers are!" I had no desire to do this, but once I started I made a list of fifteen philosophical questions.

Then a funny thing happened: when I came into Ma's room, there was a lady and a boy involved in an intense angry talk. It seemed to me a non-problem: should the boy drink tea or not? I thought: Ooha! . . . all this fuss about so little. I sat down with Atmananda. Ma was lying on her cot watching everything, but she said to Atmananda, "What's all this?" Atmananda, showing all the papers with questions, said, "Ma, she has a long list of questions." Ma said sweetly, "*Bolo, bolo!* [Speak up!]" So it started. By the way, this was all eighteen years ago, so I don't remember any of those questions, but Atmananda prepared herself, held the papers up, and out came number one question!

When Ma heard it she started roaring with laughter. I was slightly irritated, but anyhow . . . Atmananda read on. Number two question. Then three and four, but not one got answered—Ma just laughed loud, played with her hair, her toes, looked out of the window; she was just laughing, laughing, laughing. This went on from question to question. I got more and more angry until about question number nine I thought: Either *they* are fools or I am—I'm not in the right place here; let me go!

Taking my unwanted questions from Atmananda, I said goodbye, and out of the room I went—straight for the Dehra Dun railway station, where I made a reservation for the night train to Delhi. It was a long wait, so by the afternoon I thought: Let me go back and see what is going on with the laughing people. I slipped in, a bit shy, as I didn't want to get nailed down, and I found Ma sitting with a crowd in front of her, giving *darshan*. She saw me, made intensive movements: Come here, come here!, pushed the people away, and made me sit down. So I sat for some time, and I must say I found it again as fascinating as before—the way she was with people. Their devotion and bowing down was strange to me, but I was caught again. From time to time Ma threw a quick glance at me from the corner of one eye, and each time, out came the laughter again.

In spite of this odd experience, I did not take the night train; I stayed the full three weeks with Ma. Now although she must have seen me several times each day, every time it was as if my appearance caused a button to be pressed and—burrrr—there was the laughter again! Well, I thought, it can't be helped. I couldn't understand why I produced all this merriment in her, and I have never asked her.

In course of time this stopped being our only form of communication. When my three weeks were up, I decided to wind up all my work in Germany for some length of time—one or two or three years—to be near this exciting phenomenon.

I believe you have written a book in German on Ma.

Yes. I was a journalist for many years and had written a few books. After I had stayed a year with Ma, I found that my daily notes, with just a little editing could be published in that form.

When did you decide to stay on?

I never decided. After one year, I said, "It's too little"; after two years, I stayed three. Then after about four years, I didn't think about it—it just happened that I am here now eighteen years.

Can you speak about the spiritual discipline?

Everyone is given their own form, but Ma stresses that we are not to speak about it, not even among ourselves—it's secret.

I see you haven't adopted any special form of dress.

I have met so many crooks in religious robes, in the West as well as in India, I have no desire to share their uniforms. I have a great aversion to uniforms. In the generation which grew up with Hitler, we were all pressed into uniforms. In the beginning I did wear a white saree here, but I found them unpractical—I always fell about on the staircases. Now I just wear clothes that are comfortable. Anyway, I do not live in the ashram but in this nearby *dharmsala*. Only two or three Westerners are permitted to live inside. I have never been fully identified with any community—I am not fully identified with this one either. I am an outside insider.

You have now lived here all these years; is it because you are still fascinated by Ma?

That wouldn't last eighteen years. It's something deeper, something impossible to describe. After I had been with Ma for some weeks, one day I said to her, "I did not come here to love you; I came to learn how to love God—to love God better through you." At that time—yes, of course—I was very fascinated by her, so much so that it tortured me to part from her at night to go to my hotel room. For anyone in her middle forties, such an experience is confusing. But I have seen this happen to newcomers of all ages and both sexes, from East and West. It takes time to understand Ma's irresistible power of attraction. It has only one purpose: to draw towards God those whose lives have but one center of gravitation.

A friend once said to me after having a first *darshan* from Ma, "You are all like fish struggling on her line." Well, that was no nice comment, but true in a certain sense. I have often thought Ma has thrown a hook into my heart—if I try to get away, it tears painful wounds. If I follow, its pull draws me nearer to her. Suddenly the point is reached when the external senses recognize Ma unchanged and the inner sense sees only the presence of God.

Perhaps one can say she awakens the ability to love in people's hearts, with the purpose of turning them towards God. I found this turning caused by her to be a revelation within me, a liberation. Fascination freed me from its compulsion. To love became a source of inner peace, of joy and hope, which is free of fear.

Ma is so beautiful because her body is transparent for the divine light which is the source of all beauty. Years ago I said to her, "I am such an extrovert that I cannot see God within myself, but sometimes I see Him in your face." That night I made a note in my diary: During the evening *darshan*, Ma glanced at me; suddenly her face, which had looked tired, became radiantly beautiful, irradiated by the inner light. For an hour she sat silent without moving on her couch. No one dared to talk. Each cell of her body vibrated in the joy of mysterious Presence. Is it allowed to try and interpret such a situation? But perhaps when Ma glanced at me she remembered my remark that morning, "Sometimes I see God in your face." And there He was, called by my loving longing to see Him.

Can you give a brief description of Ma's teaching?

She wants everyone—inside and outside Hinduism—to follow their own way, but to follow it to the ultimate goal. She is keen that Christians should become better Christians, and many find through Ma they understand the Bible better than before. This makes her happier than someone saying he wants to become a Hindu. She is very conservative, so there is no possibility of this—you have to be born into a Hindu caste.

Are you ever lonely living this new life?
No.

What are the advantages of being with Ma?
As we progress, we begin to see there is more peace, more joy; one is able to control desires, fears, the naughty mind—that is some proof that you have the right teacher.

Are you still interested in literature and the arts?
The interest is there but there is no time, and the intensity of interest has left me. If I see some modern painting—yes—I look, but the interest is on the periphery, that's all.

Do you keep up with what's happening in the world?
Only superficially—it's enough. Months go by without me seeing a newspaper. Perhaps you can tell me what's going on?

Me? Oh, I don't know either. I live 1,000 feet above Mussoorie— that's 7,000 feet up in the Himalayas—so I never know anything. We don't even have a radio, but somehow one can live without the news. I am wondering—with your temperament—if there have been difficulties in your life since you came to live in India?
How can one answer that? We don't know what would have happened had we remained in our old habits. The difficulties depend on the community in which we live, and ours is especially difficult because—as you know—Ma follows to a high degree the laws of the Bengali orthodox Brahmins. This makes communication between Indians and non-Indians—the caste and non-caste (we Westerners are non-caste)—I should say most difficult. There are always little miseries which hurt through these laws, and we get angry and there are tensions. We are not allowed to get too close to Ma because there may be food in her room, and so on. For me there is only one difficulty, and that is that I, being outside caste, cannot have such a close relationship with my guru as those born inside caste. It is the cause of much pain at times. But it may also be Ma's way of rubbing our egos, and I think she makes nice use of it.

Anyway, I sometimes taste a joy unlike anything else I have ever tasted—and I have gone through all the scales of taste. For many years it was a source of suffering that I was not allowed to live in the ashram, but this *dharmsala* is only five minutes away, so I am outside all the involvements. I am an explosive person so it is possible I would have created trouble if I had lived inside the ashram—for them as well as for me.

One last question: have you done much traveling in India?
Oh yes, lots, but only following the procession of Ma: she travels; we travel. I have done no sightseeing, though. When I came to India, you see, my time for sightseeing was over.

. . .

Kalidas is telling me a secret no one in the ashram knows: he and Uma are planning to be married. What with this and Uma's three-day "infection," they wish to postpone their interview until January. He gives me his recordings of the late Beethoven quartets as compensation.

However picturesque ancient dharmsalas are, there is something to be said for modern luxuries such as running water, a chair on which to keep your things, or an electric fan to frustrate the flies. Although this is winter and there are no flies, two nights of dharmsala life are enough, and I am not too sorry to be leaving Hardwar for the short journey to Rishikesh.

As everyone knows, Rishikesh overflows with ashrams and holy men. I have come here to meet a German woman renunciate who has lived alone in a cave for many years, but I discover that she has become such a tourist attraction in Rishikesh that she has decided to seek a "quieter" place—she has moved to Madras!

I decide to try the Sivananda Ashram. In the ashram office, I ask the gentle, orange-clad sadhu in charge whether they have any Westerners in residence, but suddenly, a young Sikh bursts in and, addressing me, announces that he must have some dollars to buy a Japanese radio, and will give me the best rate. I explain not all foreigners are American or have dollars to change on the black market. He persists. The sadhu is benign when I ask him why they allow this. Holy ashrams accept all, he tells me.

I escape with an attendant to meet a Canadian, Bill Eilers, who lives in the ashram, in a one-room apartment at the top of hundreds of stairs. Before he will agree to an interview, he needs to know more about the purpose behind the book, so I accompany him on his daily walk through the woods around the ashram.

Bill is full of advice on how I should be approaching the project. A printed card, he suggests, with my credentials on it; then people could see at once who I am. I ask, "Would a printed card enable me to get more penetrating interviews in—of all places—an ashram?" I tell him I see my role simply as an extension of the tape recorder and all I need to do is ask. If people agree to be interviewed, fine; if not, that's fine too.

This sort of reasoning is outstandingly unbusinesslike, Bill thinks, but still—he likes its eccentricity. All right, he says, we'll go back now, and I'll be interviewed. He is dismayed to find that I must return to the Government Tourist Bungalow for my tape recorder. Couldn't I have brought it with me?

It's not so easy to cover up one's weaknesses, it seems.

*W*hen *I asked at the office about these interviews, the* sadhu
*referred to you as "Bill Swami." You are wearing ordinary western
clothes, but have you actually taken* sannyas?

Oh, no, no! It is a nickname my guru, Swami Chidananda, gave
me when I arrived in the ashram in 1974. At the time I thought I
was here for a stay of six months. It was extended to eighteen months.
Now after six years, I suppose I'll be here indefinitely.

How were you drawn in the first place?

My background makes this location totally unlikely. I was born in
1925 in Canada, the son of a jeweler, and the jewelry business was
my chief interest. By 1959, I had bought all the stores from my dad,
but then I sold everything and went into the investment business. I
joined the leading local firm. It was about this time I met Swami
Chidananda—1960—as he was touring the West.

Swami Sivananda was still alive in those days?

Yes. He, of course, founded this ashram, but it was Swami Chidananda who made the impact. It was so dramatic for me that had he said, "Follow me!" there was no question I would have done it. And by then I was married with four young children. Anyway, he didn't say that, so while I retained an interest in yoga, I turned back to the world of business.

In 1969, Swamiji returned to Canada; I was now a vice-president of the firm. Before he left he said quite casually to me, "Come to India within the next few years for a visit." I started making arrangements with my partners to be away for six months in the fall of 1973. I was then forty-seven, but something told me inside that it wouldn't work—I decided to resign. The Arab-Israeli war was on, but the stock market was very strong. I just announced at the end of our board meeting the next day that I wished to retire and if they could buy me out, and so forth. It was a traumatic experience for me. The next day, the New York Dow-Jones went down twenty-five points and kept going down. Had I not quit that day, I could never have quit.

I arrived in India in September 1974 with the intention of returning to my family in the summer of the following year. I was now retired, but was not sure in which direction to pursue my life. Before I left Canada I was accepted at the Vancouver Theological School, to start in the fall of 1975. But when I arrived at the ashram and mentioned to Swamiji my plan to stay six months, he just said, "At least!" Only then did it hit me: My God, maybe I wouldn't be going back. It was the first time the possibility ever struck me. I started wondering if I'd ever see my family again.

Just before the six months were up, Swamiji called me. He spoke about the hot weather and so on, then he said, "I wanted to tell you you will be staying in India until March next year, when you should go back to see your family and then return for my sixtieth birthday in September." It was his diamond jubilee celebration. I managed to ask, "Will my return here be temporary or permanent?" He replied, "It isn't clear to me yet; we'll talk about it again."

Well, we never talked about it again until I was leaving to get the plane to Canada—he said, "You should make arrangements to return for an indefinite period." That was the first I knew about it. So here you see me.

What were your family's reactions to all this?

I left them at first under false pretenses—that was why I wanted to go back after the first six months, to feel honest inside. But when I arrived back they greeted me as if I was coming back after a visit; no one had the slightest idea I might go back to India. My wife was upset when I told her, yet I could see something had changed—for fifteen years she had fought yoga, but she now was able to accept it and that I would go back to India. She became the instrument for making it easier for everyone else. She would say, "If I can accept it, so can you."

When I left them there was no bitterness. It was a miracle, for they all gave their blessings. I should say here that even had there been enmity, I would still have left to come here.

May I ask if you have received any form of initiation from Swamiji?

I had taken initiation in 1960, during his first visit.

Do you spend much time in meditation?

I don't know how to answer that.

Would you prefer to tell me how you pass your day?

I'm like a widow looking after my room. I cook my own meals; occasionally I attend a lecture. I will go for months without reading; I will go for months without any formal meditation. . . .

You are not expected to follow an ashram discipline?

This is a strange ashram; everyone here does his own thing. If you talk to Simonetta—she's Italian and I'm expecting her to call—she has been here for years, but she's a follower of Krishnamurthi and she calls herself a Buddhist. I am a Christian, although I study Vedanta. There was a Mohammedan here who died a year ago. This is a remarkable institution. And once you are accepted, there's no charge. It is free psychologically, also.

But like most ashrams, it must be supported by donations?

Yes, but there's no pressure to donate. A person is given permission to stay if it's considered he will benefit by his stay in the ashram. They are a bit short of space these days, so it's very much more difficult.

Does Swami Chidananda teach some form of meditation?

Not to me. He has never told me what to do or how to meditate.

He has left me alone. But he is the embodiment of compassion and thoughtfulness. He is often away for long periods, but in the early days, when I needed support, he supplied support. As time goes on you need less support; he then withdraws his support. The love is never withdrawn. He teaches by example.

Are there any basic teachings?
Sivananda taught: Be good, do good. That's fifty percent of yoga. Chidananda teaches: Be happy, make others happy.

What is taught at the lectures you sometimes go to?
The yoga *sutras* of Patanjali, Indian philosophical history, *bhakti* yoga, comparative philosophy, yoga *asanas*.

Are you not expected to put them into practice?
They used to ask Swami Sivananda, "Why don't you have a meditation routine?" His reply was, "Who can meditate?"

I was under the impression that a bell used to be rung at 4 A.M. and the ashramites were supposed to meditate then.
Nobody ever turned up.

Why, then, was it listed in the daily schedule?
Because somebody wanted to conduct a class, it was made available. Even now there's a meditation class at 6 A.M. Every night there's *satsang*. It's an active place, but there's no compulsion. In other ashrams you are expected to attend their programs. Here you attend if you feel like it. They don't want you to use the place like a hotel, but if you fulfill the objectives of this institution, they are happy.

I presume one has to be a vegetarian?
Yes. One hundred percent. I have been one since 1960.

When you first arrived here, how did you spend your time?
At first I used to travel with Swamiji—and that's all the traveling I ever did in India. I haven't even been into Rishikesh for two years. In those days I was on a routine: up at four, several periods of one-hour meditations, yoga *asanas*, study—one thing after another. I would take a daily walk, but by the time my head hit the pillow at ten, I was out like a light. Coming off an active business life, this was a life-saver. Now I spend my time learning how to do nothing. It's one of the best spots in the world because it's not easy to relax with

all the noise: it's noisier than the middle of a city. But if I ever go back, well . . . I'm living a cave-type life here, but not with my ears.

Can you see yourself going back to the West and liking it?

I could go tomorrow, but whether I ever will, I don't know. Sometimes I think I won't be fit to go back until it doesn't matter if I go back or not.

Did Swami Sivananda write many books?

Many? He wrote two or three hundred—he was writing continuously. He was a repetitive, and—by English standards—a poor writer. But I want to tell you that I only read half of one book, and the power of that book settled my mind into accepting what I'm now doing. He was basically a *jnani* yogi, but he wrote about health, philosophy, Vedanta, so many subjects. He was so generous that they used to call him "Givananda" instead of Sivananda. Someone said he was heart from head to foot. His many books are poor reading, but they are power-packed. Scholastic books read well but do nothing for you; his do.

Have you learned Hindi since you came here?

I make a joke about that. After being here for six weeks, I knew twelve words. Now I've been here six years, I know six words. But then everything in this ashram is given out in English—the books, the lectures—and Swamiji speaks excellent English.

Do you ever feel lonely in this solitary life?

It is the inner life alone that supports the outer life. No. At times I am conscious of having little to do, but it somehow has a rightness about it. As I never get bored, I don't feel lonely. I have said to my guru several times: I cannot understand my life—it makes no sense that someone with my background should be sitting in an ashram. But then when Swamiji visited my family a few years ago, one of my sons asked him, "Is Father getting what he's after?" Swamiji apparently replied, "He has already got it. He's living the life he wants!" Swamiji told me this for a purpose.

But could you not live this life with your family?

I believe everything is to a purpose. There's no such thing as a spiritual life without austerity. By far the best type of austerity is that which life gives you, not that which you impose on yourself. Life has separated me from my entire background. Here I do no fasting—none of the usual austerities—I am just here with the noises and all the other things jarring to Western senses. That in itself provides all the austerity I need. If I were to walk away from what life presents me, then I would have to take on—or life would give me—some other form of austerity, and that might be even less pleasant. We should all be content.

Now can I ask you a question?

I've asked you so many, how can I refuse?

In these interviews, are you leaving off before you ask each person the number-one question, before you dig right down to where they really are? All our social contacts are surface, but the readers of your book will want to know where your people really live.

You have raised a good point—yes—but can anyone really say where they live?

I don't believe anything anyone says; people say what they want to think or what they want others to think. You have to get underneath all that; you have to scratch deeper.

I don't quite see that as my role. I should tell you I have resisted doing this book—perhaps for selfish reasons, as I loathe traveling. I pushed the idea away two years ago, but it seems right to me now. I also know some good will come out of it. When I was forty, I decided I could never do any more work unless it was of some benefit to others. I have lived that way ever since. So although I do see your point, I feel the book will fall into its own place, and the interviews will also flow the way they have to, without anything I have to strive to say or do.

My experience with people is that they all live in a dream world. I agree with you that you have no right to disturb that illusion. But to probe in a sensitive way until you get down deep into the true meaning behind the words each person uses, well, that's what I'm suggesting.

I do understand all that, and this surely will stay in my consciousness. The idea behind the book is to find out if Westerners by coming to India have come any nearer to God, to realization or fulfillment. But can I ask that question coldly, directly from each person I meet?

I think everything else meaningless.

Perhaps. But won't the way each person speaks about his life give an adequate picture for the reader to draw his own conclusions? Is it really necessary for me to get the knife out and scratch? My guru taught me: Don't be the doer! So what comes from each person should come of his own accord and it will be right.

But should not your first concern be the audience, the reader?

Right, and that's why I have started going from place to place, although meeting people I would normally never come in contact with has its own satisfaction and reward.

Now look, you just go on without losing any sensitivity, but if the person holds back, your next question may make all the difference between a successful interview and a mediocre one. Most of us respond to questions if we are asked, but don't usually want to talk about ourselves too much, unless we are on an ego trip. It's a matter of being tremendously interested in what you are being told as a fellow seeker. The questions you ask are genuine, so your sensitivity will tell you if you are probing too deeply. This book will live only through you and your dedicated interest in every person you interview. Each person's story will have to be the most important story in the world to you—don't forget: his story is the most important story in the world to him! He thinks about it all the time. To get that story out in its totality, you will have to have that same interest. He won't resent you having a genuine interest in him. So all I am saying is: don't quit before you've won. Jump in without fear.

All right . . . I am going to jump. . . . Now you tell me, what's the purpose of your life? That's the last question.

The purpose? Well—yes,—that's good. Hmm! When you're living by yourself, all the time some thought will absorb your mind. Then you let it go. This is wise—in life you can't hold on to anything. Lately I have become absorbed in the idea that my entire mental process is geared to one thing: the avoidance of pain. Human beings are always seeking happiness and trying to avoid pain. The aim of my life is simply the avoidance of pain. If we are able to do this our basic nature *is* happiness—happiness is what's left over.

But wouldn't that be considered a rather selfish aim? If we look at the lives of the saints, they are full of sacrifice for the sake of the happiness of others.

True. A selfish man cares only for his own personal gratification—until he sees that this destroys his relationships with everyone else. It then becomes less painful to become considerate to others. What we discover by becoming less selfish is really an enlightened self-interest. By avoiding the tremendous pain of total selfishness, we suffer less. We choose the lesser of two evils. The more enlightened we become, we see it's in our own interest to be less self-concerned. By making painful mistakes, we learn. Eventually we are driven into a changed life—the new life. It is a less painful way of functioning.

Don't you think that as we are drawn into the new life, this enables us to accept the usual pains of day-to-day living? Anandamayi Ma says she is always happy because she rests in God's will, therefore everything is right. Nothing is painful to her.

That's not contradicting what I'm saying. Why does anyone rest in God's will? Because it was too painful—disastrous—to rest in his own will. Don't take what I've said as a negative statement. The mental process is a continual effort in trying to avoid pain. Sure, the final way to avoid it is to rest in God's will and let go. Here is where we become free—totally, recklessly free. We have let go of the concern for our mind and body, to rest in our inner nature. Of course this can be tremendously dangerous if preached to everyone. The hippies did this, but went to rack and ruin.

Eventually everyone has to learn that to avoid pain, one has to let go. One starts by saying: I am going to trust God—everything must be His will. Then a stage comes when we are unconcerned, we rest in our inner nature. Finally, we become the witness of whatever the mind and body are doing. But I still contend we can only be driven in this direction by the desire to avoid pain at every stage. Through bitter experience we learn it is too painful to be sinful, too painful to be selfish. So I see it as a positive approach to my purpose of life, this attempt—this obsession—to avoid pain.

· · ·

Bill breaks off to make me a hot drink. He has given me much to think about.

There's a loud knock—a dramatic contralto with basso profundo undertones is declaiming the horror of Indian bus travel: the awaited

Simonetta—Roman, aristocratic—is back from a day in Dehra Dun. The aria continues, molto staccato, into a brilliant cabelleta on the Tortures of Ashram Life.

We have all been waiting for the sound of a car outside which would announce Swami Chidananda's arrival for satsang, but I turn on the tape recorder, *molto rapido.* . . .

"I keep telling and nobody is believing—when will you writers tell the truth? . . . that ashram life is hell! I am also telling—but I know you will never write this—it is not one hell: it is five hells—five! And I can name them all—I have experienced them all. Through all the ashram hell regions have I passed! Is your recorder taking all this down; it's working?"

I tell her it is, but there's not much tape left.

"Very well. The continuation can be tomorrow."

Bill, so practical, so helpful, is disgusted at this further sign of my inefficiency. I am busy trying to cover up my weaknesses when the sound of a car is heard, and that is our cue to rush out to the hall like the tail end of the triumphant procession in the first act of Aida.

Swami Chidananda is already sitting, serene, eyes closed, ready to give his satsang. He is filled with light and joy, and has the most ascetic face I have ever seen, but I can't wait to hear whatever Simonetta threatens to let loose the next day.

Now, as I was trying to tell you last night, ashram life is never portrayed honestly. It is the protectiveness of the disciples—protecting the guru, protecting the system—that is at fault. We all know about the blissing-out part. Who ever writes about the frustration/ego-smashing side? There are some marvelous people who are naturally spiritual; there's no effort, there's great simplicity, great humbleness. They don't have to go through the conflicts and excruciating tests we have to go through. *We* are going through hell; *they* have bypassed it. The truth I am saying bold and loud!

Perhaps devotee writers feel it is their duty to sugar-coat the life-in-the-ashram pill. Before you take me on a tour of all the ashram hells, can you tell me how you landed up in this ashram?
I came only for Swami Chidananda. I met him in Paris in 1969.

He was attending a conference. I had just left the Catholic Church for the Russian Orthodox, and my priest was so open-minded that, as he knew I was interested in Hinduism, he took me to see Swamiji. I had only been converted for one month. The moment I saw Swamiji walk into that crowded room—I don't know what happened—it was all finished. You cannot explain this sort of thing; you have to pass through it.

Swamiji was the embodiment of everything I dreamed of: the love, the light, the purity, the beauty. I heard all his talks for the next two days. It was a bewildering experience. Then he disappeared. I looked for him everywhere. I could not find where he had gone. Swamiji just disappeared out of my life.

Now, I was a very famous fashion designer, and I had a contract with a chain of stores in America for the previous eleven years. I had to go there for publicity tours twice a year. I was breaking away from all that so I could concentrate on the work in New York: fashion shows, interviews, and so on. My contract was finishing in June 1970, but when I arrived in New York, they wanted me to go to Chicago and San Francisco also. Fashion didn't interest me anymore, so I didn't want to go to California. But in New York I called up the Divine Life Society to see if they knew where Swamiji was. He was in San Francisco! So my contract—which was to be my last in America—brought me to Swamiji again.

Swamiji returned to India in December 1970, and I flew back to Paris to wind up my affairs. By January first, I was with him in India. I didn't know anything about the ashram. I came only for him.

But why do you find ashram life hell?

I don't find it hell—I find it *five* hells. Are you listening? The most obvious hell is the lack of minimum comfort. There are buckets of water, and like policemen who have dates for changing into winter and summer uniform, we have dates for hot water in winter. It can be freezing, but until a certain date, no bucket of hot water. Then we have lovely noise, and dust, and food that comes in which you have to heat up—that's if the electricity is working and the stove hasn't busted. Here the power fluctuates with much enthusiasm, so everything breaks. There are the pigeons who like doing their nests in the fuse box, which also makes it dangerous to interfere with their strange habits.

There is always something *extraordinary* happening. But all year round we are sure of one lovely unmovable fixture: the food is the same—rice and lentils with a bit of vegetables. At least we are able to boast that food has no longer any importance. Oh, my God, there are *so* many hells! The animals—we have zoos in our rooms: monkeys and famished dogs trying to get in; ants, scorpions, cockroaches and flies already installed inside; mosquitoes, having feasted to their fill, wanting to get out. Oh, I forgot the wasps. They also come in to nest. We have to get accustomed to all this. And I must not forget the mice. They are very small, and as no doors fit properly or touch the ground, they stroll underneath. You suddenly see a gray thing that has the cheek to stare at you—and he is not even afraid.

But then there is a much subtler hell, a more difficult hell. It is having to live with other people. You have to get along with them and not indulge in likes and dislikes, not to get caught up with emotions and sensations generated by them, but to relate to them in a detached way. We are collected together for the same reason, but from different backgrounds and cultures. It takes much patience to look on everyone as your brother or sister.

Now do you begin to see what I mean about the hell regions? The more I go on, the more hells come into my mind. Another is—these reflections are all personal, for we are all at different stages of evolution, yes—the loneliness of ashram life. Suddenly you find yourself living in a community with people you don't know and people you would never have even met in your ordinary life. There is lack of communication; it is not easy. In this solitude comes the lesson—most important—how to live with yourself and not depend on people and objects.

Would you like to say something now about the benefits of ashram life, or something about Swamiji's teachings?

Swamiji doesn't give any teachings—that was my big surprise; he only gives silence—at least to me. Let me begin from the beginning. Having worked for twenty-five years in fashion, I couldn't see myself sitting on the banks of Mother Ganga doing nothing. I asked Swamiji if I could look after the orphans. He never answered. I had even written to him about this from Paris. Silence. Silence. Silence. By the end of 1972 I was rather demoralized. Someone suggested I try looking after the lepers. I was so wanting to work that lepers and children were all the same to me. Swamiji said I should draw up a program and join him in the south, where he was on tour.

This ashram is surrounded by three leper camps, mostly beggars cut off from human contact, rejected by society. They were waiting for death, passive, sad. I made up a program and joined Swamiji. He never looked at the program; he never called me. I was to fly to Paris, so at the last moment he pulled out the papers, but said there was no time to discuss it, so many devotees were waiting for him. He suggested I extend my visa and wait for him at the ashram. When he returned, together we visited the lepers. We started by taking away all the begging lepers and put them in a camp; Swamiji then measured symbolically the first rations. From that day, that group never had to beg. They have food, medical care, and clothing.

At the camps we started handicrafts—they weren't obliged to work; it was absolutely voluntary. I then flew back to Paris, where I got rid of everything (I had already sold my fashion house after the first trip to India). I was back in the ashram a few months later, and from fashion, destiny gave me lepers to take care of. I took care of the medical side; there was no compounder, no dispensary, no doctors, nothing. I learned how to give injections, medicine, dressings; it was not easy for me. The dirt—the most horrible wounds that had been neglected, rotting; the sweet smell that never left you, worms eating away mutilated flesh, eyes eaten away by white ants. It would have been impossible for me to have done that work unless I had devotion and love for Swamiji. He was working through me; I could have done nothing alone. Only now can I tell you, as you have asked—that was Swamiji's teaching.

Later, when everything got settled in the camps, and as I was still full of illusions and believed a guru should give so-called spiritual instruction, I started going to someone else for Vedanta instruction. I love philosophy; I am not really a *bhakta*. I heard Krishnamurthi and was fascinated with what he did with people's minds—he takes the mind and puts it on a higher level—so I decided it was time for me to look for gurus and teachings. I went to the Himalayas, everywhere from Sikkim with Karmapa, to Kalu Rinpoche in Darjeeling, and from Swami Mukhtananda to Krishnamurthi, who became my obsession. I even had the nerve to go to a great lama and tell him I had come to learn so that I could understand Krishnamurthi better.

May I ask you who you consider your guru or gurus?

First, Swami Chidananda, who opened me up to spirituality—and I must say whenever I'm in front of him I am a total idiot. I can only say: Yes, yes, Swamiji, yes. Secondly, my other guru is Krishnamurthi, who for me is the living Buddha—he is unique. I am very lucky. I have had a lot of gurus; whoever teaches you something is a guru. All my initiations have been from Tibetan lamas—Swamiji has never initiated me.

Now I should tell you what Swamiji told me years ago: "This ashram is your spiritual home in India. You can leave your things here. You can travel and do whatever you want, but remember this is your home." This is what has happened; I have traveled all over this country, but I always come back here.

Bill told me yesterday you are building a house in the ashram.

Only yesterday Swamiji gave the blessing on the plot of land which had been chosen in 1973.

I see in this room of yours you sleep on the floor and use the bed as a table. You must have lived a very different life before you came to live in India.

Different, it was. Italy was discovered as a fashion center after the War, and in the fifties and sixties I had one success after another. I was practically the queen of Italian fashion. I was constantly traveling round the world. I had everything I wanted: beautiful houses, luxury which I adored, success which I adored, and I made a lot of money which I adored. Then came the change in my life.

In 1962 Christian Dior died. Capucci, the Italian designer, opened a fashion house in Paris. It was a success, so he persuaded my husband—who was also a fashion designer, Alberto Fabiani—to also open in Paris. In Italy we had separate houses: his was Fabiani, mine, Simonetta. But we merged our businesses in Paris next door to Balmain, Dior, and other big houses. More success. But Paris became the bridge to the East. Our marriage broke down—he was always flying round the world one way, and I was flying the other way; we never met.

I was a tremendous success, but all alone. I had three choices: to go to a psychiatrist, throw myself in the Seine, or take to yoga. I met a *hatha* yoga teacher, and for several years he helped me. But of course, when one starts meditation one's life begins to change; the things that had appeal and glamour fall away. I started going to the Russian church. I had always reacted violently against my own church in its hypocrisy, its system of banging fear into children—fear of hells, fear of heavens, fear of sins. It's disgusting what they do! For many years I couldn't step inside a church.

Do you want me to leave all that in?

For me you can put in anything that's against the Catholic Church—I am *violently* against it. With great difficulty I am only just getting over it.

I ask because . . .

Yes, yes, I know one shouldn't, but I'm still very violent you see; I still have strong feelings about this. When I was fourteen or fifteen, I had great spells of fear, and it took years to get rid of. That is why I have such resentment against the Church.

Would you rather talk about the positive side of ashram life? I'm sure there's much that you have enjoyed here.

It is unique as an organization. We have lovely monks. It is a bit like a seaport; people come and go. It's good for beginners, as there are lectures, a library, three-month courses. Residents are allowed to follow their personal *sadhana*. It doesn't matter from which country you come if there's a deep involvement in the search for the inner life.

Since I came here, Swamiji has drained me of all my love—I can't love any more. He has taken it all. I think of him as a fisherman throwing his net all over the world in his travels and catching new fish to bring to the path. Only after many years did I understand what he taught me—there are no teachings, but he taught through his silence.

I have also found that we must learn to be aware of everything during the day; that is a form of meditation. Meditation does not mean to have a rosary in your hand and have your eyes closed. It means to live here and now, to be aware of what's happening inside and outside. Krishnamurthi gives what I call teachings: clues and directions, how to look at ourselves, at things. He gives no conclusions; on the contrary, he puts questions with no answers.

Do you keep up with what's going on in the outside world?

No, no, no! I don't read newspapers anymore. The only books I read are on philosophy. At first I couldn't stop reading—it was like a folly. Now I read much less. All books say the same thing: practice! Through practice, I am finding out, the doors open slowly and you get a glimpse that every teacher is showing you the same way in different words.

Bill gave me a lecture last night, so I am going to plunge deep. In your old life you had much fame, wealth, happiness, and much misery also. Now, in spite of the ashram hells, have you made any inner progress?

Progress? Many times I've watched a fascinating thing: we are always the same. We don't change. Maybe with realization there's a complete transformation. Through our practices we become aware of our emotions, and look at them, but they are there. They are more quiet; they are sleeping instead of awake. So what is progress?

Well, should you have to go back to the West—would you be able to re-adapt?

It would be a good exercise. I do go on short visits and arrive peaceful, calm—until one has to meet other mentalities, problems. You see that the East has been teaching you; now the West is teaching you; you are always given teachings wherever you are. Once you can take all teachings under all circumstances, then you know you have arrived. But once you have lived in the East and you have loved the East as I do, it is extremely hard to even think of ever living in the West again. You see, I have one big wish left—that is why I have asked for that tiny house here. I want to die in India . . . to be burnt here and have my ashes thrown into the Ganga.

Apart from this wish, do you have a goal in your life?

There is no goal.

Why are you here?

You start looking for the goal, then you learn there's no goal. There is no seeker, there are no teachings, there are no teachers.

That sounds like Krishnamurthi.

Yes—yes—yes . . . but you have to understand all that. The path is divided in two: first is the ego trip—one wants progress; one forces oneself into all sorts of disciplines. But all that's the trip of the ego. Second part: we come to realize there's no "I"—we are just energies; there is no goal; there are no teachings.

You say we are energies, does that mean you don't believe in karma and reincarnation?

I am studying all that, meditating on what reincarnates. I don't believe in a stable entity that reincarnates. It's a mixture of energies that at a certain point crystallizes into a human being, and with death, they dissolve. What reincarnates, I don't know. This is my Buddhist training and ideas. We are still in the field of the mind, so we each project and receive within the field we are working in or believing in.

But isn't spirituality something apart from the mind?

We speak about spirituality as a thing which can be acquired. It is a gift. All spiritual experiences are given as a gift; we do not achieve them. The spiritual life is to get rid of the ego, the "I," and to wake up perception and intuition. We all have that potential within us. But for Westerners especially, our minds are so clear, quick; our brains are working all the time. We function through the mind, not the heart. *Sadhana* means to get out of the mind so that perception and intuition can develop.

It's a slow process; people come to India searching, searching. It's so hard to judge what's in their hearts, if they are only frustrated, or afraid of life, or of facing responsibility. There are so many problems.

Do you have a problem with your family? Do you ever miss them?

At the beginning my mind wandered from the East to the West like a pendulum. But one has to pull it back into the here-and-now. My son was only sixteen when I first came here. It's an extremely long process getting rid of everything: attachments, material things —they grasp you. It's not enough to say: I will throw everything away! They cling to *you*. Mental detachment is all right, but the practical part takes time. It is not difficult for me to stay here; I was never at home anywhere in the West.

At the beginning when we started talking about the ashram hells, I left out one important hell. It is a hell that lies in store for us. It is the hell waiting for us if we ever go back to the West. You see, we suddenly find we do not belong there. That can be a traumatic shock—we don't know where we ought to be, who our friends are; so much has dropped away—old habits, our old way of living, the old way of thinking. We find ourselves as alone in the West as we are in the East. Yes, one may now have a lovely hot bath, some chocolate, all the things one used to love, but they have lost their meaning. Clothes have lost their meaning; all the things one cared for have lost their meaning. The taste of the West after many years in the East is a *serious* hell because it attracts and repels at the same time. The only way is to find the famous "middle way," the way of detachment.

. . .

I am back at my home in Mussoorie. I now have four interviews but no photographs. I will have to go back for those later. (Bill Eilers had chided me greatly for this further sign of incompetence.)

Before leaving for Anandamayi Ma's ashram, I had written letters seeking interviews in various places; most are unanswered. There are only two positive replies. Swami Satchidanand—he signs himself: "Ever your Self"—says Mother Krishnabai will be happy to welcome me to Anandashram (the ashram of the late Swami Ramdas). And General Joginder Singh in Chandigarh—he is a sort of secretary/ devotee of Sant Gulab Singh—has given me a date next month. Sant Gulab Singh is over a hundred, and has one American girl disciple who is especially close to him and has served him many years.

These two signs are hopeful, but one is in the south of India, one in the north. So the question is, what to do in between? My wife says just turn up at all the places you intended to go to and do your best.

The next day, our wise and gentle Swiss friend Swami Jnanananda gives me more of this same advice. He has walked up the hill from his forest retreat to visit us, and he tells me, "Do this book as part of your sadhana—selflessly—and you will see: as you go from place to place you will be guided to those who are already marked to give the interviews."

Perhaps it is my apprehensiveness about traveling that holds me back. In the past, wherever I have gone in India, I was accompanying my guru. As part of his entourage, I was just to follow the arrange- ments made by others: "Get on the train please," or "Here is the car for you to ride in," or "This room will be yours." Swami Jnanananda understands all this, and he encourages me. I see that he is right, and I start packing. I sort out my cassettes and begin studying the ashram map of India.

But before I leave on my search for the already marked and chosen interviewees, I walk down the hill to a nearby village. Here, in a simple hut enveloped in peace and solitude and surrounded by woods and superb views, lives our Swiss Swami friend.

S *wamiji, the last interview was given by the Duchessa Simonetta Colonna di Cesaro; she was so volatile that she started her story in the middle and gave the beginning at the end. So if you don't mind, could you start at the beginning? Of course, I know you are Swiss by birth and have lived in India continuously for nearly thirty years—but can you tell me something about your past?*

For anyone who's renounced the world, there's no past.

Were you not a musician in your early life in Europe?

I was never a professional musician. I had a deep interest in music, but from the age of fourteen I was inspired by Eastern teaching. Even then I wanted to come to India. At the age of twenty-three this was realized; I came, leaving Switzerland and my past for good. I have never gone back.

When you said there was no past, what did you mean?
At the time of initiation, the guru absolves you of your past, hence a new life—you enter the new life.

Did it take you long to meet your guru?
One week.

Oh! You must have heard about him before coming here.
No, no!

But how did you find him? Coming to India in those days at the age of twenty-three wasn't so common.
True. I had never heard of anyone who had done it. So many tried to discourage me, but as soon as I arrived here everything happened. The guru actually expected me—he knew I was coming on such-and-such a date. I didn't know myself. He told a disciple a person would arrive while he was away and to ask him—me—to wait three days. I waited. I could have chosen between two persons—each could have been my guru. But my natural inclination drew me to the person who kept me waiting.

Where did all this happen?
Calcutta—Dahkshineswar.

How long did you stay with your guru?
Twelve years—as long as he lived. After he left this world, I never returned to Calcutta; I stayed in the Himalayas. My guru took me each year for five or six months to Rishikesh or Hardwar and gave me a place by the Ganges for meditation. During those twelve years I spent all my time by the banks of the Ganga.

Can you speak about the spiritual discipline he taught?
He taught Kriya yoga. He insisted on regular practice. Along with renunciation, discipline is essential. There must be regular practice of a guru-given technique and mantra. In order to realize these practices, I was drawn to complete renunciation; it is the best way to have sufficient time and to leave off thoughts of the world.

How did you support yourself?
The guru took care of me in every way. He blessed me for the future, and he's still taking care of me now.

You haven't mentioned his name. Was he connected with Parama-hansa Yogananda, as he taught Kriya yoga?

His name was Swami Atmananda Giri. His guru was Swami Kev-alananda, Yogananda's Sanskrit teacher. But my guru, Swami At-mananda Giri, actually took *sannyas* initiation from Yogananda.

How old was your guru when he left the body? As you were still so young, did you feel the need to go to another guru for instruction?

He was sixty-eight. No, no, there was no need! He told me how to carry on; he told me before his passing.

Did you wait long before taking sannyas?

Three years. First I lived in the ashram as a *brahmachari.*

Can you give an explanation of sannyas?

We belong to the order known as Dasnaami sannyasins, which was founded in the ninth century by Adi Shankaracharya. *Sannyas* means renunciation; it is the fourth ashram in Indian culture. The first is *brahmacharya*—student life. The second is *grahastha*—the house-holder's life. The third is *vanprasta*—the life of retirement from worldly pursuits. The fourth is *sannyas*—the life of complete renun-ciation dedicated to the teaching of divine knowledge. The four di-visions can be described like this: the first is one of addition, for a student must acquire knowledge. The second is one of subtraction, for a householder supports his family. The third is one of multipli-cation, because having retired from the worldly life one has nothing else to do but acquire inner knowledge. The fourth is one of division; that is the time to distribute these inner riches for the enlightenment of others. So really to enter *sannyas* means to dwell in God.

You are non-Indian, non-Hindu, non-caste. Are you accepted by other sannyasis?

I have not only been accepted, but legally also. There are some orthodox sections that may not accept this, but those in authority do. I became a *sannyasi* according to Hindu rites.

When you say legally, what does that mean?

It has been attested by the court, by the government.

But why?

The guru said it would be of some use.

Are you an Indian citizen?

I deem myself so. According to a Hindu law which is now not in vogue, by entering *sannyas* I automatically become a Hindu. As it's not the prevalent law, I abide by the present rules. My foreign nationality has stayed all these years, and I get a yearly visa which is a formality, nothing more.

Can you speak more about the teachings?

All spiritual teachings are the same: the essence is to dwell in God, to dwell in the Reality at all times. By spiritual practice, one aims to lose one's little self—to become one with the Ideal.

Do you accept disciples and teach?

I pass on what my guru taught me when there is a demand.

But you do have disciples.

There are some people who call themselves disciples. These teachings are in the traditional line, but specifically adapted to the individual. Beside the technical aspect of yoga, one has to pass on the subtler aspect which leads to the ultimate transformation of each person who takes to the teachings. No two are alike. The exact nature of the teachings cannot be disclosed. It is beyond any words—call it grace, God's grace! To pass on grace, and to be receptive to grace, that is itself grace.

In the early days did you have to study Sanskrit, or did your guru teach in English?

He spoke to me in English. But there was not much talking. He asked me to practice what he taught me. Studying the ancient scriptures was my own liking; his emphasis was on regular meditation, discipline, the remembrance of God. It was not a question of study from books to add to one's knowledge. It was to surrender to the Divine, to feel what is meant by Reality or Absolute Truth. To feel this is to know it. Such feeling comes by intense self-giving. It is the grace of the unspeakable power of the Divine that opens the way to bestow the new life.

Earlier you mentioned our backgrounds, hinting perhaps at our karmic destiny. Would you say it is this that causes us to be drawn to a particular guru?

Everything is due to past determination. There must be sincere longing, sincere prayer—plus God's grace. It is that grace and the blessings of some good soul. Such good souls are everywhere in the world. The blessings of a good soul in the West may help a person to go to the East.

Swamiji, can you say something about the five thieves—lust, anger, greed, attachment and pride?

They are known as the five thieves because they steal true happiness; they take man away from the eternal joy which lies in Reality. These thieves are the deluding factors, for man easily gets identified with lust, anger, greed, infatuation and ego. All spiritual practice is to enable us to eradicate these evils. Otherwise, there's no meaning in any practice. Holiness, purity, is when we are transformed and these evils have no existence within us. When they are unmasked, love shines forth.

What are the outer signs of a person who has controlled these thieves?

He is detached. He is detached even when they are present in his environment. Attachment to the five thieves is due to ignorance. Detachment is due to knowledge.

What advice do you give to people wishing to break away from these thieves?

If they haven't yet found a guru, they should pray to God ceaselessly for a guide. After finding a guide—a teacher—they should serve him in any way they are capable and follow the teachings as far as possible. If one does not have a guru, one at least should cultivate the company of good persons, seekers of the way; one can learn much from them.

Would you say it's essential to have a living teacher?

I would say so.

These days there's no shortage of imperfect teachers. How can sincere seekers avoid falling into their hands? Or is there no such thing as an imperfect, false guru?

If one is false the guru will also be false. In the guru-disciple relationship there are many obstacles, the greatest being doubt. There will be persons questioning the disciple: How do you know if your guru is realized, if he's competent? They try to awaken doubts—and should there be doubts, this is not a true disciple. Personally speaking, I found that the guru who happened to be guru to me was much better, more evolved than I was, so it was to my advantage to follow him. One follows the guru because one wants to follow God, and if one is sincere in following God, then the guru will become the instrument of God.

Also, it is not a question of my guru and your guru and someone else's guru: there is only *the* guru. "Guru" is a state of consciousness—it's not a person. The person is only the instrument through which the power of guru flows. Hence to say "My guru" is belittling the guru. It's also the cause of much confusion.

Would you say there's any advantage in studying spiritual books or scriptures without having a living teacher?
Yes, they prepare a person for more personal guidance.

Is it essential to receive initiation from the guru?
That depends on the guru. To have a guru usually means one gets initiation from him, but some gurus don't give formal initiation. It depends entirely on the guru's will.

What should be the aim of the seeker after Truth?
Truth.

You spoke about the importance of meditation. Can you speak about the meditation you practice?
It all depends on the guru's instructions, which are usually given in secret. But essentially, meditation means to quiet the mind—more than that, to quiet oneself. That means to be silent in mind, body, feelings, thoughts; above all, to be steady at heart within, for at heart "thou art." To be steady in the innermost center of one's being or consciousness, practice of equanimity, practice of renunciation, practice of the remembrance of God are essential. Then alone one can take refuge in the innermost silence. The state of being is beyond silence itself. It's inexpressible.

Swamiji, do you still sit at fixed times for meditation, or do you consider your daily activities as meditation?
No. The particular time to meditate is one of the conditions laid down by the guru. It should go on indefinitely, irrespective of any thought that one has realized or not realized anything. But of course, the whole day should be spent in practicing the presence of God, practicing the presence of that Being.

Do you sit at any particular time?

In the early morning—it's called the hour of Brahma—four o'clock till sunrise. This is traditionally the time when yogis and *sannyasis* practice meditation. The difference between a beginner and an adept is that for the beginner it's an effort, for the adept it's natural.

Again, would you say this naturalness comes from our background inclinations?

Every sort of practice becomes natural in the course of time. But here we are dealing with the intrinsic nature of one's own self, one's own being. So one can say that when meditation becomes one's own nature, it is natural.

Like most sannyasis *you wear simple orange cloth. Do you consider this important?*

This sort of uniform is helpful in the beginning; it's like hedging a small plant, because like this, one is not troubled by the world. One ultimately outgrows the color. One ultimately outgrows all outward signs. In the life of renunciation, simplicity is foremost.

Do you observe any rituals?

None of my own; sometimes I observe the rituals of my friends. To place a flower in a vase is a ritual. One can make one's whole life a ritual without making it a rite. Everything can be a ritual if all one's actions are offered to God. A ritual means to commune with God.

Is it possible to be married and live a spiritual life?

In the path I am following, marriage is not advocated. It is a way taken after one has done with the world. But generally speaking, marriage is no obstacle on the spiritual path. Most *rishis* and sages of bygone times were married.

If a young man wishes to take the path of renunciation, how should he overcome sensual desire, which is instinctive?

That path of renunciation is not advisable for young people: it is advocated in exceptional cases when the guru through insight knows it is possible. Generally, one should pass through the life of a householder, but on reaching a certain stage, retire from the worldly life —it can be done along with one's wife—and then devote one's time entirely to the spiritual life.

Is this practical for those living in the West under the present hectic conditions?

I cannot say what is happening in the West; it is the natural evolution of man that he should retire from material involvement when he grows old, wherever he lives. Otherwise the purpose of life is unfulfilled. Family life, earning money for a reasonable living, doing good for one's country, et cetera, is called *dharma*—good actions. This one should do. But above all, one should know how to retire from these outer actions, because the inner life also has a demand. The later stage of one's life is for contemplation—everything becomes subordinate to realizing God.

Now you have asked me about the hectic conditions under which most people live in the West. I believe the time will come when only those who meditate will be able to sleep at night. The total dependence on money and the security we imagine it brings is total ignorance if we are afraid to be alone, without material possessions. At the time of death even millionaires are alone—nothing outside can help us. We are alone with our fears if we are rooted to the body, and we carry those impressions with us into the Beyond. Those who have meditated will also be alone when they leave, but will be filled with peace and they will carry that peace with them.

To forget the world makes man a pilgrim; to forget the next world makes him a saint; to forget the ego gives him self-realization; forgetfulness of that forgetfulness is perfection.

Swamiji, that's extremely moving, but can these profound teachings be applied by those living in the West?

In truth there is neither East nor West—there is one humanity. These teachings are Eternal; they propagate the Eternal; they help humanity to realize that which is Eternal. Man's involvement in materialism is an experiment; he plays with nature and nature plays with him. Gradually man wants to become the master, so he puts away his toys and looks towards himself to find a marvel—there is no greater creation than himself. He can then probe the mystery of his own being, and it is here that the Eternal teachings come as a guide.

So anybody anywhere can follow such teachings. For someone like myself, India seems to be the place for this life's evolution, but that does not mean that those who yearn for the new life cannot find it in the West. We should go beyond the names and forms they represent and arrive at the nameless, the formless Truth that has Its being everywhere. It is universal understanding, universal realization, complete identification with the higher life that alone brings salvation to Christians in the West as well as to Hindus in the East.

Can you see yourself ever living again in Switzerland?
Switzerland is within me.

Swamiji, when I first asked you about these interviews, you said the idea was good, but would I be able to get at the truth? What did you mean?
Very few know the truth.

Exactly, but can you say how one gets the truth?
If you are in quest of the truth, you cannot get the untruth. Life changes for everyone; while living in this life, we are to start the new life. The new life has to become the real life, then only is it to be mentioned as something auspicious. Otherwise, the new life may change into a newer life or even change back into the old life. The question is: Who is living? What is life? What is the aim of life?

As you go on collecting these interviews, try to get at the truth by asking these questions. People often ask me why I have chosen this path. From my early days I wanted to know the purpose of life, what one can attain within a lifetime. If I become an artist, what is the ultimate art? If I become a poet, what is the ultimate poem? If I become a musician, what is the ultimate music? I tried all these things; very soon I realized there is no ultimate. So then I wanted to know the purpose of this life which is made up of so many moments. What is a moment of life, a moment of consciousness, a moment of existence? And as I was asking these questions—I was living in England in those days—I was asking: What is time? The reply was: We have no time to know what time is. Then my thoughts went to the East, for traditionally it has always been the place where people have found time to inquire into time.

You see, I didn't find any purpose in this life. What to do? Whatever one achieves, is there an ultimate satisfaction? Now I will tell you because I know you were a musician. I went to London to enroll at the Royal College of Music. They said, "You are too old!" That's strange, I thought, hardly twenty and too old, . . . already one life gone. It was only when I met the guru that I understood. He told me, "You first look for God, then everything else will be given to you. We are all running after the lights and delights of the world, not realizing we are sacrificing God Himself."

Can you expand on what you were saying about inner calm at the time of our physical death?

Life can be beautiful if enriched by inner silence, what you may call silently loving, silently feeling, silently thinking. Such a life fulfills the purpose of life. That is to live correctly. If we live correctly, we are able to face death fearlessly. That incident in life known as "death" we have to face without fear, otherwise death becomes distorted and we cannot pass through it in peace. So if we find the right way of living, the secret way of dying will be revealed. Death is the door through which we pass into life renewed.

Although I know you live this solitary life in peace with yourself, are you ever lonely?

There's no such thing as loneliness. One likes company for the sake of spiritual discussion, for the sake of *satsang*, for the give-and-take which is part of life. The reason why there's no such thing as loneliness is because when one is alone, one is alone with God, and when one is in company, one is in company with God.

Can you say something about this one-room dwelling which only has a bed, some books, a corner fitted as a simple kitchen? Have you been here long?

The owner of this estate met me when I was living on the banks of the Ganga. He suggested I should try the solitude of the forest. Reluctantly I came here. At first I stayed only a few months at a time. It has become a bit like a permanent abode. When I am here I manage everything myself. But a *sannyasi* is homeless—it is one of the conditions. The whole world is his home, and as such, he is not bound by any one place. Living this simple way has never been a problem because everything had to be given up, everything had to be forgotten.

We should never forget—those of us who have been drawn to live in India—we are living here by God's will. The spiritual life is the beginning, the middle and the end of all life; everything is subordinate to the spiritual idea; everything else is a play. I found the one great difference between the East and West is that in the West everything of this world seems real, whereas in the East one sees everything is a play, and only God is real.

Now I think we should stop. You should eat some food here. As you know, I only make rice and lentils, but I am happy to share them with you.

There is no need, really.

Look, I have to eat, you have to eat, you can join me. This is what I eat every day. It must have taken you an hour to walk here.

Well, I have brought some biscuits and fruit . . .

Good. We will share. Today God is giving us a feast.

.   .   .

Swamiji walks me part of the way up the hill back to Mussoorie, still giving advice. He has reminded me that an interviewer should not talk about his own beliefs unless asked. Every disciple believes he has the greatest guru in the world, so he is unlikely to want to know about yours anyway. Swamiji's advice is invaluable. From today, I resolve to see myself as an extension of the tape recorder; I am to float along, enjoy. I must have no expectations and make no comparisons. Whatever happens will be right.

The next morning I am at the local bank asking for traveler's checks. The manager smiles: the bank is out of them; it will take a week. So it must be that I am to leave in a week.

Meanwhile, as I am sorting out my things (though it is cold in Mussoorie, it will be warm in the south), we have an amusing visitor. He has lived in India many years, passing through many ashrams, and all of this history has made him an eloquent—if biting—raconteur. He agrees to let me record his reminiscences, which go on at such great length that only about a third can be included here.

BILL AITKEN
Landour
Mussoorie
20 December 1980

According to my birth certificate, I was born on May 31, 1934, in Tullibody, Clackmannamshire—the smallest county with the biggest name in Scotland. Our backyard ran straight up to a mountain 1,375 feet high. I remember sitting there listening to the drone of the universe and watching the sheep—I was antisocial from an early age. I hate cities and love mountains, so, Malcolm, this is why I have taken the trouble to struggle up here to see you.

My father was a coppersmith, but he moved to England, so I was educated in Birmingham and at Leeds University, where I studied comparative religion. My professor was a Baptist minister who—in spite of himself—liked Hinduism; he was, however, disappointed when Hinduism charmed me more than his own Baptist line.

I was going into the church as a minister, but I was too honest— I didn't have the call. I was all set to come to India as a missionary to teach. I was doing an M.A. in Indian philosophy and mysticism, one of those airy-fairy refined nonsense courses that modern universities in their learned ignorance specialize in. As a student, I went conscientiously to the services of every denomination each week—I had holy communion with the Quakers, the Mormons; I went to the High Anglicans, the Low Anglicans—Leeds has everything.

Now I had been brought up as a Presbyterian Calvinist, but it was one of my professors who answered my question: Was I cut out to be a Christian? A guest speaker from France who was a faith healer gave a moving sermon. I was thrilled. Because my Presbyterian professor was in the chair, at the end of the sermon he officially denounced it as against the Presbyterian beliefs. I forget what they are now, but I thought: Well, if that didn't move you brother, then you have no bowels to be moved. It was then I decided to look elsewhere. I was in my early twenties; I turned more toward the Gandhian studies.

I loved Yorkshire, and Leeds had marvelous symphony concerts on Saturday nights. I must have heard you, Malcolm, when you were playing in the Halle Orchestra with Sir John Barbirolli.

Yes, I was in the orchestra in those days.

In those days, the only thing going on in Britain was Bertrand Russell, and he seemed rather dry. For three summers I went to the island of Iona—there was a Social Consciousness Christian community there. But in those days, I liked Gandhi's teachings the best.

When did you actually decide to come to India?

After I did my M.A. I felt a filial obligation towards my parents, so I took a teaching job to be near them. But as I was an indignant Scottish nationalist, I would wear the kilt and never stood up in the cinema when the national anthem was played. I had this pointless rebel instinct which just wore one's own psyche down and achieved nothing. As for teaching . . . No! Life was beckoning me—there's more to it than being a faithful son. And the world seemed to be in a mess; I wanted to do something about it.

My friends all said: Forget it; nothing will change. The Director of Education said: Don't you know if you leave at twenty-four you'll commit professional suicide—what about your pension? I thought: God brought me into this world. He's beckoning me. He's not saying: Your pension, my boy, first get your pension! It was then I decided to hitchhike round this fabulous world wearing the kilt. I passed through the Middle East and was to return via Australia and America after staying some time in India.

I arrived in India twenty years ago, but somehow never got round to moving on. I found my guru, so eventually I became an Indian citizen.

Were you looking for a guru?

Not consciously. When I arrived, I was taken up with the Vinobe Bhave movement; he was walking all over India collecting land for the landless. I walked with him for six weeks all over Assam, until my health broke down. I took a job teaching English in Calcutta, but during the vacations, I started visiting ashrams. I was drawn by the teachings of Ramana Maharshi, and in Calcutta, I met Arthur Osborne, Ramana's biographer. I stayed with him at Ramana's ashram; there I got a taste of ashram politics—Ramana had left the body in 1951.

I also went to see Sivananda—a huge man—but although I accepted his hospitality, I came away criticizing him, which was mean.

But Bill, what did you intend doing with your life? Did you just fall into this thing of looking for a guru?

No. I was a big-headed academic gangster trying to get big qualifications with as little work as possible. My idea was to go back and be respectable, teach, nothing more. Though I would have said, "No! No! I am looking for God; I wish to offer myself." I always had a monkish trend, and my father called me an idealistic prig. I never liked organizations; my way was to go against the stream. So after I finished in Calcutta, I went to stay with a similar type: Sarla Devi. She won the Bajaj Peace Prize only last year for her Gandhian social work.

But before that I realized that if I were to stay in India, I had better learn Hindi. I came up here to the Landour Language School and stayed with the missionaries. It was hell, these prim and proper London suburban ladies telling me Buddhism is all wrong and Hinduism—the four thousand years of Hinduism—is lived in vain. How could they know? When an Indian Christian *sadhu* came, they wouldn't let him in. Hilarious people; the end of the Raj.

There was something about yoga and yogis that appealed to me, and before I left England, I was told about an Englishman who was living as a yogi in the Himalayas. He had been a professor at one of the Indian universities. He changed his name to Krishna Prem and was living in an ice cave miles from human habitation. Actually, I found I only had to walk a mile from the bus stop, and there was a comfortable, well-established ashram almost like an English country club. And Krishna Prem, far from being a shaggy yogi with long matted hair, was more like a beaming English curate with his shaven head. My first impression wasn't too good—but he was to become my *param* guru. My actual guru—Ashish Maharaj—was also there. They were both English, six-footers, sticklers for Hindu ritual, and they were both dressed in orange.

They immediately floored me every time I opened my mouth. I asked if I could stay, but after they gave me lunch, they escorted me out. I took away a negative impression, but even then they had been my mentors; they recommended I go to the Gandhian school run by an English woman disciple of Mahatma Gandhi—Sarla Devi.

She came to India in the late thirties. She is one of the few people I have ever met who sincerely practices everything she preaches. Her preaching is austere: up at 4:00 A.M., even in winter, bathing in the mountain spring, not eating salt—the typical Gandhian faddist diet. It was a terrific introduction to village India—not typical, because the nature cure thing was taken to excess. When I joined my guru's ashram four years later, Ashish Maharaj tried the usual persuasion to get me to eat salt. I thought Sarla was right, but he said, "Look, you are now living here doing *puja* to Thakur—Thakur is the deity—and *he* likes salt, so you better like it too!" I am still learning to find a balance; I am one of those awkward customers who swims the wrong way.

You haven't said why you left Sarla Devi.

There was a sexual crisis in my life, and in the Gandhian movement it is all *brahmacharya*, a distorted sense of celibacy. Celibacy has much to be said for it, but obviously God has given one sex for a reason. Anyway, I was running into embarrassing possibilities, and the crisis came when I hovered between life and death with typhoid. Sarla treated me homeopathically, and I fasted for forty days. I was about to peg out—I had bequeathed my sleeping bag, the only thing I possessed—when I had an extraordinary experience, the sort of thing one reads about the medieval mystics—all is One and One is all.

It completely opened my eyes: life is not what we are taught it is —it isn't the rat race. We are taught by people who don't know what it is. They mean well, they haven't *seen*, that's all.

The scales dropped from my eyes. I saw what a glorious thing human existence is; I experienced this engine of the cosmos beating by the crude force of Eros, and there is nothing to be ashamed of. But as soon as I recovered, I lost it when I started eating—I had received this experience in an out-of-the-body state. I knew I had to find it again. Gandhian ideals were fine, but now irrelevant to me. I had to move on. This tantalizing glimpse—call it divine; it was real —changed my life. I was going to be a wandering *sadhu*. It sounds like bravado, but that's how it was then.

I would rather die in a ditch looking for this—I was telling myself—than stay on doing good work changing others. Then Sarla said, "All right, become a *sadhu*, but first go back and get advice from Krishna Prem; he's lived like that for years." She, being a social worker, could not bear *sadhus*—she regarded them as bums. So this was like a communist advising one to confess to a priest.

I walked the thirty miles across the hills to the ashram. Krishna Prem was the only holy man of any denomination I have ever met who treated every subject as fair; nothing was taboo. His mind was a mirror of nature: nothing is small, nothing is great, nothing is good, nothing is dirty. We talked. My ideas and beliefs were crushed; I was punched into the ground. He was just telling me, "You are running away: you ran away from England; you ran away from Sarla; when are you going to stop running? You are standing in your own light!" I was knocked down, kicked in the ribs and stamped upon.

Then I was shown my room. It was ten at night, end of March, snow falling, 7,000 feet, no bedding, a wooden bed with a mat. My aim being to become an instant *sadhu*, I only had the clothes I stood up in. I can still escape—I started consoling myself—this is no place for me; I am misunderstood! But common sense told me if I did, I probably would never see morning.

One of the things Krishna Prem told me was that wandering *sadhus* are lazy; the whole of their lives are devoted to looking for their next meal; how can they do *sadhana* or serve God? He also told me to go back to teaching so that I wouldn't be living off anyone, but to do meditation and keep at the inner work.

When the body is frozen, common sense arises. In the morning, a much subdued Bill went to Krishna Prem, and said, "What you told me is right." He replied, "Before you go back and get a job, stay for a few days—you can help in the kitchen."

This was the last six months of his life. Staying with him was the greatest privilege in my life. He had no hang-ups; he understood everyone's deepest feelings. He reminded me of the dervish who was asked, "How is it you understand people's problems without them explaining anything?" He replied, "My mind is still, like a clear lake; they look in and see their reflection." That is the whole thing about the living guru: you can't get it from any book.

What happened after that? You worked in the kitchen?

Yes. I was given three books to study: Blavatsky's *Light on the Path;* Ouspensky's *In Search of the Miraculous;* and Herrigel's *Zen and the Art of Archery.* The story of my life was encapsulated in the last book. It was at times hellish living in the ashram.

But you were told to stay for a few days. How long did you stay?

Seven years! Seven years!

All the time in the kitchen?

All the time!

What happened when Krishna Prem passed away?

I was given initiation by Ashish Maharaj, his successor. He is also very British, but when he came to India, he also never went back. First he went to Ramana, whom he describes as the shining sun because if you sit in the sun's presence you are warm, but when you move away, you lose it. He wanted the give-and-take of the guru-disciple relationship; this he found in Krishna Prem. All this was about 1942. He now teaches himself, although he's not interested in what he calls "stamp collectors," those jumping from ashram to ashram.

What were the teachings?

Traditional Hindu. This included dream analysis, which was re-discovered by Freud and Jung. We had to take the study of our dream life seriously as being nearer the real realm than the physical. There was work on the farm—or in my case, in the kitchen—from 6:00 A.M. till 10:00 at night without a break.

Didn't you have to take part in the rituals?

Yes. There were three *aratis* a day, and I had to make the meals for Thakur and offer them to him.

With your stormy nature, was it not difficult to accept a guru and ashram discipline?

The idea insulted my whole being, but call it the grace of God or whatever, I came to see a strict guide was necessary. And obviously you never choose anyone unless you fall in love—trust and love are close. In choosing a guru, you have to be bowled over first.

Can you say anything about the spiritual disciplines?

Gosh, you'd have to define "spiritual." Realization and the world are the same; it's the mind that divides: this is spiritual, this not spiritual.

What was your daily life like, then? Can you say?

Murder! Really, because there I was, a foreigner, having to do everything in an Indian mode. The agony of sitting on the floor with rickety knees trying to make my *chapatis* round. My guru was like one of those harsh Zen masters; he believed in throwing one into the deep end to make you swim. On the first day, Ashish said, "You make the chapatis." I said, "All right, you show me how to make the first one." He said, "If you want to learn, do it!" I started making shapes like South America or Iceland. I was disgusted. I had to learn.

How many Westerners lived in the ashram in those days?

In 1965, only an Australian boy and myself. I was in the kitchen; he ran the farm. There was an Indian couple and Ashish, and that was the entire population. Fellow disciples came and went, of course.

How did you get on with everyone?

I should have thought that was self-evident. Such dramas. Such Brahmanical rituals and laws—this hand to be used for this, that one for that; don't let your shadow fall on this, total awareness of how you eat, ritual bathing in freezing water. There were all sorts of tantrums, explosions and emotional heartburn, feeling sorry for oneself, and wanting to stab the guru and run away. Life in an ashram brings out every gamut of human experience and emotion.

But you stayed all those years. How did you maintain yourself?

The four years I spent with Sarla I worked as a handyman, in the garden, and so on. One's expenses were small, so they were met by the school. But what could you buy apart from toothpaste, which was frowned upon—and soap, which was also frowned upon. One washed with *reeta*, a local fruit, and cleaned one's teeth with soot. For the seven years in the ashram, I was given an honorarium for service to Thakur, who would also pay my bus fare once a year for a holiday in Nainital.

Bill you have been here twenty years. How did you adapt?

I am still adapting. My breakthrough into Hinduism came when I stayed with a Punjabi printer in Allahabad who took me for the customary morning bathe in the Ganga. It was winter, chilly; we stripped off. I could see flotsam and jetsam and cigarette cartons and all sorts of muck bobbing about. He plunged in, calling, "Come! This is Ganga Mai." "You don't expect me to jump into this," I yelled. "It's filthy!" He replied, "It's not the water that's filthy; it's the dirt."

Suddenly, like Zen *satori*, I knew he was right. I jumped in too. And from that moment, I've never had typhoid or those things. I've had immunity—psychic immunity. You can't stay in India on boiled water; you have to come round to the Indian way—if you get a bug, it's for a purpose. It's easier to live that way, too.

Lama Govinda must have lived near you at the ashram.

Yes, he was a dear man, the most Buddhistic of men. His wife was different. Lama would invite you for tea in a mild and scholarly manner, but the wife would brow-beat him. She never butted into his scholarly activities, though. They were so beautifully dressed in their Tibetan costumes that the local residents used to say that before setting out for their evening constitutional, they would turn to one another and say, "Do we match?"

There was another great character living nearby, Sunya Baba—Sorenson—who left Denmark in the thirties and came to India as a landscape gardener.

Was there anyone else besides your guru whom you admired?

Admired? Don't say admired—I feel love is the only touchstone that rings true to all men. So did I love anyone else. Yes. I fell in love with Prithwi, a fellow disciple, and that's why I left the ashram. I had my guru's blessings, for he said if I couldn't find what I was after through love, I should give up. So I am now following that path.

I left in 1972 and have no regrets. As you know, I work as a private secretary to a Maharani.

One thing my guru taught me when I started this: I won't promise you anything, but you start on this and you will never have any regrets. He never lauded anything: This will be seen on the inside; that will eventually be attained—but whatever he said has rung true. The teachings have been right for me.

Have you found an inner peace you didn't have before?

Am I less prickly than before? I suppose with age. . . . It's just a fact of life; you give up writing to the editor. I'm just as awkward as ever, but it's less apparent. Stir me and I suppose it will all come up again.

Do you still meditate?

Not in the sense of sitting down and conjuring up nothingness, but in the sense that one is all the time reminding oneself that one is here for a purpose—to see the One behind it all. So, no formal meditation. In the ashram one sat all night in special postures, strapping oneself up; all that jazz. What is it all about? Even in trance states, does it change anything? You zoom up, but then you have to come down.

Can you see yourself ever living again in the West?

Because I was put through the excruciating ashram mangle—the washing machine—I could live anywhere. My guru taught me the inner path is facing things you have always been afraid of facing. So he said, "Get back into life, have a bank account, pay income tax. How can you understand the One that encompasses all when you are terrified of the irritating aspects of the establishment? Conquer the establishment, be part of it, then say it's not there. There's no less the One in the market place than in the ashram."

So thanks to my guru giving me the boot, these last nine years have been as excruciating—that was the mangle; this is the rolling machine. I couldn't care about going back to the West—I could go to Soviet Russia, having read Solzhenitsyn and how he managed to stay cheerful. I don't say I would succeed, but equanimity would be there in the face of drastic change.

In this age of enlightenment, the West has lost the validity of the inner search. In India the inner search goes on—you can talk to almost anyone here and he will not think it strange if you say you have come here to be with a guru. India has managed to retain a balanced attitude towards possessions—renunciation is a mental attitude, not a forced dropping of everything. Indians are just as acquisitive as Westerners, but they don't have the same attachment; they don't cling and are not in such a mad rush to achieve. The real India is the inner India, so *that* you can carry away with you. It's nice to have the hygiene and comforts of the West, with all its efficiency, but not if we forget what we are striving to have them for.

. . .

I am packed and ready to leave. I have the traveler's checks. I have fifty cassettes bulging out of all pockets. The distant snows of the Himalayas are shining as I listen to Kate's last words of encouragement. As I start my long walk down into the town, a tourist taxi (odd—in December) is passing, and I am given a lift down to the Mussoorie bus station, which saves me an hour's walk. An auspicious sign.

The journey has begun.

Part Two

When traveling in India, you carry a bed-roll or sleeping bag. The latter is my choice, and I need it on the night train to Chandigarh, for—even in first class—Indian trains provide no bedding. I do have the compartment to myself, though; but it's all relative, since I can't sleep!

We arrive in the dark, and it's still dark when I reach the home of General Joginder Singh, who had written me that welcoming letter. He and his wife proceed to show their love for their guru, Sant Gulab Singh, by showing extraordinary kindness to a stranger who has invaded their privacy; they give me a room, make me breakfast, then drive me to the house where their guru lives and where I shall meet Radheshwari, the American girl I have come to interview.

I am taken straight into Santji's room. He is sitting up in bed eating breakfast and looking not at all his age, which is 104! He beckons me to sit on the edge of his bed, takes my head into his outstretched hands, and kisses my forehead gently, sweetly. Then he hands me a piece of his toast, but takes it back to put more jam on it.

Radheshwari brings tea, so now I am having a second breakfast. There's no talking, but you don't have to talk in the presence of such a saint; the saints talk by showering their love on whoever comes to them, even if it's in the middle of breakfast. I can't help laughing, laughing because of the great feeling of happiness and light that has descended.

Radheshwari is also laughing quietly. She has been enjoying the divine mystery for a number of years; I can see she has been scooping up lots of love-toast.

Radheshwari has lived and laughed with Sant Gulab Singh so long that she now speaks English with a pronounced Punjabi accent; she is his only Western disciple, and she is with him twenty-four hours of the day, looking after his physical needs. He is extremely deaf, so hardly any talking is involved. She is there to serve, to let in the few devotees who call, to pass the tea and shine.

Every evening, Santji is taken by car to the Chandigarh rose gardens, where he walks for a while, then calls on a few of his close disciples, just like a father visiting his children. He has never had a large following, and has resisted having an ashram organization grow up around him. Once, when offered an ashram by a rich devotee, he replied, "The real ashram is within your heart."

My interview with Radheshwari stretches over two days and is constantly interrupted. But Radheshwari is always calm and loving and cooperative.

I was born in Los Angeles and raised in Long Beach, California. I was attracted to an introspective life rather early. My family was upset—yes, quite upset—that their daughter would hide away in a cell and never come out again.

To whom were you devoted?

To Christ. My family did their best to make me go to parties and mix and, you know. . . . But it acted the other way, for when I looked around, I saw there were other ways too, other beliefs. I saw the Unitarian Church, and they invited Zen monks, yogis, and followers of other religions to speak. So you see, when I decided to come to India to find an enlightened saint, my family was not surprised—they knew my inclinations.

I suppose you found most Indians surprised at a young girl leaving her family.

Exactly. But at least my family is happy now that I have found what I had been longing for.

How did you make the break and come to India?

I had a wonderful job as a dental assistant earning much money for a girl of twenty. I was with some top dentists on Hollywood Boulevard, but when I started looking at my colleagues coming every day, taking the money—what for?—I said: Let me see some other life! At the end of the sixties, some of my friends—they were poets and artists—had been to Europe and described the life in Spain as much quieter, simpler. I saved the money for one year in Europe, and although I met so many interesting people, it seemed to me that everyone was in search of another way—a *real* way of life. So a few of us got together to go to India to look for an enlightened being. I had meditated on my own in Europe, and although I had all the time, I knew it wasn't working on my own. I knew I had to find someone who could show me.

How did you travel?

By car. We were firm in our goal. We had talked it out and decided that on arrival in India, we should split up, as the guru meant for one would not necessarily be the guru for the others. We were idealists—there were five of us and we loved each other, but we knew that being attached to each other wouldn't do us any good. We were like children, and said wherever our hearts pull us we should go, and only in that way will we meet the saint who is to help us.

Did it take long to find your prospective gurus?

For some of us, no. One French lady went to Swami Muktananda; she stayed years with him. The Englishman stayed with a saint for a year and kept *maun*—silence. I went to a yoga ashram near Poona; it had a huge library. There—along with learning hatha yoga and raja yoga—it prepared me for the Indian way of life: how to dress, how to eat, how to behave. But even though there was a great mystic soul who helped me—he appeared in my meditations—my heart told me: You have been helped, but now you should move on. I continued the search in Rishikesh, where I met several saints, but they weren't for me.

I received a telegram from one of the five friends, asking me to come to Delhi. Here I met a Baba, so we all traveled to Simla, where I stayed for some time. That was an interesting personal opening for me. During my morning meditations, I would literally cry, "Oh, God, show me your saint; I am here all alone; can't you send somebody for me?" Even throughout the day, my heart was so intense with longing that when I went out, I could hardly hold back the tears.

After one month, I met a lady who kept saying, "My Santji is coming to Simla; you should meet him"—just like that. When he arrived, she did take me—it was Sant Gulab Singh. He was giving an informal talk to a few devotees in a house where he had been invited to stay. As soon as I saw him, I was like one struck. I thought: Oh, now *there's* someone! All the doubt, the sorrow, the confusion vanished—I was in supreme joy.

It sounds too perfect, doesn't it? But this is how it happened—and just as soon as I came into the room! I couldn't understand a word of what he was speaking; I just sat at his feet watching him. He was glowing, throwing out waves of love and compassion. When he became aware of me, he opened his arms wide and called, "*Ao, ao, ao!* (Come, come, come!)" He was smiling, and his cheeks were red and glowing.

Was he speaking in Punjabi?

Yes. And it took me a good six months before I could understand.

How old was Santji then?

They say he is about 104 now, so he must have been just over ninety then. It's a miracle in itself that his memory for the scriptures is still so sharp, and that he can read without glasses, besides having perfect recall of many thrilling events from his past. You know, he still quotes from the Gurbani in Gurmukhi, from the Gita in Sanskrit, and from the Koran and the Persian Sufi mystics like Rumi and Hafiz in Persian. You have seen him walking without help, even at his age.

Radheshwari, you have been in India so many years, how do you manage to support yourself?

This question I often wonder about myself. To think of it is enough to send one into ecstasy—it's perhaps the greatest miracle. I had an abhorrence of working for money; there's joy in work, so working was all right. But to be handed money for it I felt was insulting, especially if one puts one's heart into the work. But here in India one has a goal—one has come only for God: one hasn't thought of the body, so He has blessed the body with its daily needs. I am lacking in nothing.

If you think of it, Christ said, "Think not for how thou shalt be clothed and how thou shalt eat; does not thy Lord know thou hast need of these things?" I was so filled, crazy with the desire to find Him, I never thought about these things. Rather I thought I would prefer to be without than to be chained to a weekly pay packet. Do we really need wall-to-wall carpeting? I have had to do without so many things for a number of years, but there has been a joy in the heart and fulfillment in the life.

Sri Pad Baba, who I hope you will meet in Vrindravan next week, was an inspiration for me. He had nothing but a blanket to wear. I had nothing but one little bag with a change of clothes in the early days. Oh, it's all coming back to me. . . . At one time I only had a *dhoti* to wear, and when I washed it in the river, I had to dry it on my body in the sun. I lived like that for eight months—Sri Pad Baba's influence was so strong.

These days, everything I wear has been given to me because the devotees see I am serving Pitaji day and night. The simple food we have always gets shared by whoever comes—you have seen that yourself. I can't see that I'm in need of anything more.

And Santji, how is he supported?

Supported? He's just sitting in the lap of God! He doesn't depend on anyone.

Can you tell me more about the miracles attached to the photographs of Om Baba, Santji's guru, and why Santji gave me eight this morning?

He explained that should you come across anyone suffering or in trouble to give that person a photo. I have never seen him give eight to anyone; it must have some meaning. But I can tell you I have seen the most incredible miracles happen through Pitaji giving this small photo. But he usually gives them directly to each person who comes with a serious problem, and he asks that the photo should be placed in a locket and worn round the neck. I have seen so many return to tell him their sufferings or problems have vanished, or if not vanished at least that they are able to accept and live with what troubles them.

These small photos have such power you don't even have to wear them. My own mother suddenly became ill and thought she was having a heart attack—all that I am going to tell you I heard this October when she came out here to visit me—she only hinted in a letter that she was ill. They took her to hospital and found it was spondylitis; it was so advanced she couldn't walk. The doctors told her they would operate but she would never be able to walk again.

She wrote to me lightly about it, but I felt there must be something serious. I told Santji: "Mummie appears to be ill"—just like that, nothing more. He gave me a photo of Om Baba to put inside my letter to her without telling her anything except: "This is Om Baba"—nothing more. She started getting well, and before she came to see us she was climbing mountains in California. She was so happy to see me with Santji. . . . my happiness made her happy, you see.

Do you ever think about the future?

A few years back I started thinking about security. A devoted person offered me space on his land to build a little cottage—this was up in the hills. We talked to Santji about it. His reply was, "Why are you planning? At this stage, you can't even imagine what will happen to you—leave off these ideas; you are going to be happy wherever you are!" I let that chance go. Since then, I don't even think about whether I will be allowed to stay in India or not—sometimes there's trouble getting a visa. Pitaji annihilated *all* desires, this way, that way.

I notice that sometimes you refer to Santji as Pitaji.

Pita means "father," and if one uses *ji* with any name, it gives it more respect. Most of Santji's close devotees call him Pitaji. He calls us all *bacche*, "children." It is out of love—and such love he has!— that we call him father.

Although you are so integrated here, you can hardly ever meet any Westerners. Do you ever miss Western society?

Things are in the heart; one remembers sometimes, but through grace one never hankers after anything. You must remember, when I left the West I was fed up with everything there; I don't have to go through all the boring list of horrors going on then—and perhaps they are still going on. It has taken me ten years to start seeing the good side of the West again.

Like you all those years ago, many others have taken the road towards the East hoping for a better life, yet many have not found the inner peace and fulfillment you have. Is there a reason?

The reason is the destiny of each person. There is a definite benefit in seeing the world—even the Indians should see America—we should see it all, feel it all, and know that life isn't just the customs within the society into which we are born. Many have been to India and been disturbed by the dirt and poverty, the climate, and endless difficulties. That had to be for them. Others see beyond that, to the beauty; then a stage comes when we see beauty everywhere. But one cannot fight or alter one's fate.

Do you find it difficult to adapt to the conditions?

At first I wanted to look like an Indian lady, but it's hard even though you keep to the customs, because the Indians themselves see you as a Westerner. The girls here can't move about unchaperoned. I wanted to be free to travel; I soon found that as a Westerner I could. It's important not to upset anyone by wrong behavior—we're so free in the West—so I learned to always cover my head in the company of holy men, and so on. It was four years before anyone would give me a room in Vrindavan—they were just not used to seeing foreign girls on their own. No Indian girl alone would ever be given a room. So sometimes one's foreignness helps.

Do you see this life you have with Santji as the end of your search, or could you still go on?

Both. I could very happily jump right out of this body now, yet I see there's far to go. Scientists are discovering that the Creation is endless—so much to be discovered had been covered, hidden. But what about He who created all this? Is He not as endless and full of mystery to be unraveled by His devotees? As long as life is, there will be mysteries. I have become happy—why?—because I know whatever I need, He gives me.

Do you still have any goals?

The one goal is Him. What He wants me to do here, He will make me do. At the moment, it's to serve Santji; until he leaves his body, I will stay at his feet serving him. After that, well, that's the beauty: I don't know. But I do know I'll never serve another as I have served Santji. About five years ago, I arrived back from an exciting trip with

Swami Jnanananda—Pitaji was so happy to see me. He was laughing
at the great mystery—you see, he is not at all possessive. I was sitting
with him all alone. He never speaks personally to me, so we sat in
silence, and suddenly a flood-wave came on me—visually—and I
blinked my eyes. A rainbow of color showered over me, glittering
light; I couldn't see Santji through it. At the same time, my body felt
cool, refreshed but exhilarated—and joy and joy that was vibrating
bliss! Then came to my mind what Santji had said a hundred times,
"All the eighteen places of holy pilgrimage are found at the feet of
the guru!" Since that day and that experience, I never wanted to go
anywhere. These sayings in the scriptures aren't just words. Someone
has experienced them just as I had experienced what it means to be
at the feet of the guru.

*In the two days I have been here, you appear to be in a constant
state of divine intoxication. But do you ever have moments of
sorrow?*
We are not above our moods. Sorrow comes. But that too is as
precious as everything else. It's in the depths of sorrow—the dark
night of the soul—one gets the greatest revelation of His love, His
grace, His mercy. And when you cry, "Oh God! God! Are you there?
Show me! Show me!"—and you are in enough pain, that is the blessing
of blessings. I have had my share of pain. Being a lone woman is no
small thing. You have to find Him. I have seen Him come when you
need that love. *Then* there's that ocean, endless ocean of Light. Without words God will tell you, "I love you, I love you most: I am waiting
for every cell of my own self to come back."
So that is what I have been given here; it's the firm foundation of
faith. This is *His* body; He will do with it as He likes; I'm to watch.
As it's His, He must take care of it. I found out that secret through
the greatest moments of pain, when I had no one else, nothing else
to lean on: no source other than Him. Is it not a wonderful life to
know that?
Pitaji has shown me two ways. One, to pray in a humble way for
God's grace to come. The other is to accept everything as it is and
know He wants it that way, and if you love Him, why question His
wishes? Until we find the guru, the world is the guru. We learn like
that—even the wind will teach us.
When I first met Pitaji—within four or five days—we were sitting

alone in the sun at Simla. He said, "My child, name anything you want; just tell me." I was thrilled all over and started weeping. I couldn't speak. I knew what I wanted, but how can you say you want God? But what was on my mind, having just found Santji, was staying in India—the visa. How could I stay? This was on my mind, but one cannot ask for a worldly thing. I stood up and shouted in Pitaji's ear, "God! God!" But he replied, "No! No! He is already yours; ask for something else!" Tears were still falling down my face, but I couldn't say anything more. Of his own accord, Santji turned to me and said, "Look, you can stay as long as you like in India. If it's some papers, we will arrange that—you are not to worry; we will keep you."

So you see, he gave me that. I am not in need of anything else.

. . .

Santji is being taken to General Joginder Singh's house; this serves a double purpose: he will be able to see his loving children and I will be dropped home. Santji comes into the house and gives a ten-minute discourse to an audience of four—he rarely speaks to larger gatherings. When he gets back into the car, he clasps my hands to say goodbye. I ask him to bless the work on this book.

He kisses me on the forehead again and says: I have asked God to bless you!

I leave Chandigarh a few hours later on the night train, in such high spirits that the descent into the confusion of Delhi hardly affects me. There I must collect a three-page itinerary from the travel agent; it's a nervous traveler's panacea for all ills—replete with name and number of each train to be taken, alongside much other information. It's all immaculately typed-out in duplicate. How can anyone go wrong?

I have arranged to stay in the ashram of my guru's successor, Sant Darshan Singh. This is in Old Delhi. On the way I am thrown out of the taxi scooter and narrowly miss being run over by a bus. Fears and feelings of inadequacy overcome me yet again. That evening Sant Darshan Singh, who is a shining example of humility and kindness, actually comes to see me in my room. I tell him I feel like an orphan suddenly thrown out into the cold world. He replies, full of compassion, "Yes! But wherever you go never for one moment forget that your guru is watching over you—that power must guide and help you!"

I know this is true, and I know I am suffering from pre-concert nerves.

I leave. But it's not long before things appear to be going most definitely wrong. I am in the Vrindravan Station rushing along the platform to catch the Taj Express, which will take me to Agra; there I hope to interview a Dutch boy whose story, I am told, is of special interest. The train is on time, and I jump into the first class section. But . . . as we are pulling out of the station, the conductor rushes up to me saying all seats are full. I say I have a confirmed reservation, and take out the lovely sheets of proof. Yes, he says, checking—but for 12 January. Today is 11 January!

I am so stunned that he lets me sit on his wooden seat in the passageway. It appears one can still be hopelessly untravel-worthy, even with the most magnificently typed itinerary. I realize that I shall be arriving in Agra one day too early. My friend Pritam Singh Nagpal—an old disciple of my guru—who lives in Agra and has promised to meet me, will surely arrive twenty-four hours after I do, and in the meantime, I will have no way to contact him and nowhere to stay.

I am saying to myself that there must be a purpose behind all this; I must not be confused or anxious, but must flow with all currents, under all circumstances. I know there's a guiding hand over my head, so to be in the wrong place at the wrong time must have some meaning.

We pull into Agra. The tourists dash into the waiting coaches off to see the Taj Mahal; the porters barge in every direction. I stand alone with my sad luggage, waiting for the excitement to simmer down.

But within a few moments I am more confused than ever. Pritam Singh Nagpal is giving me a rib-crushing embrace, laughing uproariously. "Your paper is telling twelfth and here you are coming eleventh!" he shouts in my ear, still laughing.

On the way to his house, Pritam tells me how he happened to be at the station, and his story instantly erases all doubts I might have had about my future travels. I ask my friend to write down exactly what happened, and here is the tale printed just as he gave it in his own words:

PRITAM SINGH NAGPAL
Belangaj
Agra-4
13 January 1981

Respected brother,

When I met you in Delhi you had shown me your programme of reaching on the twelfth by Taj. We were all looking forward to your visit and had told many brothers and sisters about your programme. I invited them to meet you on the twelfth in the evening at my place.

On the morning of the eleventh, I was still lying in bed (fully awake), when I saw our Master with you smiling a little behind Him. And Master told me, pointing towards you that, "He is coming today—receive him at the station." And slowly the light was withdrawn. I was expecting you on the twelfth and here was a positive and clear direction to me to go to meet you. On the one hand I was overjoyed but found it difficult to tell my family.

As we were to go to the Sunday Satsang, I made up my mind to leave my wife there and then go to the station. I had to rush and found the Taj had steamed in. It took a couple of minutes to leave my scooter and purchase a platform ticket. I knew you had a first class Indrail Pass, and as the first class compartments are towards the engine side, there I made my way. You were there looking towards me. I was happy I had received the right direction from my Master—that he chose me for this small service to my brother, and in His Grace to save you from any inconvenience.

Perhaps I am not able to express myself fully, but, brother, on your journey now and hereafter on this earth plane, you are fully protected by our Great Master—this proves that much. And for myself, I am also under His benign Grace. I have recorded this in my own limited manner, but the whole thing can be felt rather than explained.

With my best regard,
Yours-in-Him,
Pritam

· · ·

From this moment, how can I ever suffer confusion, doubt? Everything is controlled. Everything is as it has to be. Everything that has to be accomplished on this venture will be accomplished.

The next morning I am taken to the historic house of Rai Saligram, popularly known as Hazur Maharaj, a nineteenth-century saint and the second guru of the Radhasoami Faith. This movement was founded by Shiv Dayal Singh, who was born in Agra in 1818; since those days, there have been many splits, and the movement has spread all over Northern India. (There are thriving centers in the West also.) Dr. Agam Prasad Mathur, who is head of the history department at Agra College, is a direct descendent of Rai Saligram, and is therefore the living guru of this particular branch—though in Agra alone there are three noncommunicating branches of the Radhasoami Faith.

Arriving at the house which Dr. Mathur now occupies, I ask to see the Dutch boy who is Dr. Mathur's disciple and who lives with him. But—I am shown into the guru's presence instead. He is sitting on an elaborate bed, chewing betel nut. He appears to misunderstand the purpose of my visit, for he starts an uninterruptable discourse: "Yes, yes, a good idea, but the book should open with a historical survey of the bhakti *movement as it started in medieval India, leading up to its modern flowering last century. . . ."*

After ten minutes of invaluable but unusable advice, the learned doctor pauses to spit out the red matter he has been chewing. I take courage and point to a fair-haired young man who has just prostrated at the feet of the guru and crept to the back of the room. I say, "Forgive me, it is this boy I have come to interview." Dr. Mathur recovers quickly, "Yes, yes, of course. . . . Paul, . . . take him to your room; . . . give him a copy of my book and show him round the samadh. . . . So kind of you to come, good-bye!"

PAUL IVAN HOGGUER
Radhasoami Satsong
Hazuri Bhavan
Agra
12 January 1981

I am Dutch by birth. Although I am now twenty-six, by the time I was sixteen I had done everything that was good and bad—busy peeping my nose in all fields, always liking to be first. It had been predicted by a lady who could see the future—my worried mother went to see her—"by his sixteenth birthday he will change; you will be proud of him."

Since fourteen, I had lived away from my parents in Amsterdam. I became part of the drug culture: fast cars, fast company, boys, girls. And whatever there was to do I did, even at that age. It was hard living—many times I was moneyless—but there were many experiences. So by the time I was sixteen, I was feeling: All this is no use to me; I will go home. I phoned my parents; they said, "Let's try again."

I went back one day after my sixteenth birthday. There was a talk: "Are you willing to go back to school? Do you want to work? Please think about it." But I became privacy conscious; I demanded my own room; I wanted to think. The body was sixteen; the mind was already far away from things with which my parents were concerned. There was pressure. I must do something, *must*! But I couldn't accept anything. Daily talks about schooling, daily paper searches for jobs, all of which the mind rejected. Internally, I knew I was searching for something else.

Four months passed. My mother came up with a suggestion: Take a job in a nearby hotel. I started working as a cook. I developed an interest in cooking, so I went one day a week to school. Then my father, who is a businessman with enough money, began talking about opening a restaurant: You learn to be a chef in Switzerland, learn all the nice preparations. . . . By the time I was seventeen and a half, I had worked in several good hotels—then I happened to pick up two books by Paul Brunton.

The moment I put my nose into them there was a transformation in my brain. It was telling me: Your life is for this; get hold of it! I'm a fast reader. I finished the two books in one day and started searching for others like them. The fantasy in my mind was: You've had a past life as a yogi—you have come back to go on. At last I knew what I had been searching for. But my parents didn't welcome the news: "What's this new nonsense?" My interest in cooking dropped; I studied spiritual books. I couldn't stop reading.

One day I saw that Mahesh Yogi was in Holland, so I went to see him, as I knew I had to do something practical. I never liked organizations, but I wanted to learn a meditation technique. I even took initiation, started practicing, got interesting results, but couldn't give myself. I went back to reading—all the Theosophical books and so many others.

One day at a transcendental meditation meeting, I saw a lady. My mind said: Make friends with her; she has much to teach you. She was about forty. I was then an ascetic fanatic, unable to accept Mahesh Yogi, but knowing the real guru was waiting for me somewhere. I spoke to that lady and we became fast friends. She was a vegetarian; she was pure. She had a lot of knowledge, but she was still searching. We played the I Ching, the Tarot cards; I read her books, met her friends. We went to different groups, to Switzerland to see Krishnamurthi. We meditated together, and we dug out a lot of things.

But the day came when my mind said: She has given you all you need; she has done her job. At that moment, something came between us. She saw it. I said, "I am meant to go on alone." I told you I was a fanatic; had I met my guru then, and had he asked for my life, I would have given it. My ideal was the Himalayan yogis; I knew I had to go there. She didn't like that; neither did my parents.

How old were you then?

Seventeen and a half to eighteen. Once I started, development went fast. I was on a staircase—I had to go up. I went to forests to meditate. The inner experiences were good. At the transcendental meditations, the checker-uppers—poor fellows—were surprised. It was arranged that I could attend a teacher's course free if I would cook the meals. I never wanted to be a teacher, but I wanted the knowledge. And there I met a boy who had been to India; when he mentioned the word India, such an energy force entered me, I knew my time to go was near.

But how did you manage to come here?

I had bought my rucksack and clothes. I should tell you that for two long years at every meal there were fights with my family. There were long faces and tears.

Was that because you wouldn't eat meat?

I left off meat, fish, and eggs. There was weeping on my part as well as theirs. My father said I was mad. I would pray to God (I didn't have at that time a particular God): Why is it like this? Why can't I find my guru? Why is everyone pestering me? I sold everything I had to prepare for the journey. But a month before I was to go, I was called for an interview to join the army. It was another puzzlement. But somehow I was the only one to be rejected, surely the working of a superpower; I was free to leave.

How did you travel?

Have you heard about the Magic Bus? Lots of hippies from all countries going to India on a German bus with French papers and an English driver. Interesting. It was to leave 31 August 1974. I sat in my seat, detached. My mother had taken pills to calm herself. My father was asking me to get out. I was already like a free bird. The staircase was beckoning. If the Queen of Holland had asked me to stop, I could not.

Now a funny thing happened: my father has a big car business, and when the bus was to start, the engine failed—we all had to get out and push. The face of my father! He pushed an extra two hundred guilders in my hand, saying: "Just in case—at least take a train." But we were off, and the six weeks to India was wonderful, no breakdowns, but many stops to enjoy the countries through which we passed.

I saw a Dutch boy in the bus. My mind said: Listen to him; he has something for you. He sat in front of me. I had given myself the idea that I would no longer speak nor smoke. Up till Switzerland I never spoke, but I handed round some toffees. That boy took one; contact was made. He asked, "Are you going to India to smoke or for a spiritual purpose?" I told him. He said, "I am a follower of the Radhasoami Faith; I have been initiated for six years, but not allowed to see my guru. So, as I am on my way to Australia, I will go to Beas to see him." He then gave me a full account of the teachings.

When I heard them, I thought: Yes, I know all this—this is right. So I then told him if he didn't mind, I would also like to see his guru. I later fell asleep and saw a face; to this day I think it was Swami Shiv Dyal Singh, the Radhasoami founder. I had been planning where to go, what to do, but all this went, even my idea of becoming the disciple of a naked yogi living in a hole in a wall. I wanted nothing but contact with this Surat Shabd Yoga, as explained by this boy.

We left the bus at Amritsar—bye-bye—took a train to Beas, then a *tonga* to the Dera. I was nervous: Here I was seeing the first guru. We went inside, and the problems started. That boy did not have a letter giving him permission to see his guru. The secretary said, "No permission: no place to stay!" We couldn't even stay the night. I was more upset for that boy. This is an organization, so they have to behave like that.

It was dark outside, but we saw a tea shop. The owner heard our story and said, "You stay with me—many foreigners have this problem." It was a gift from heaven; the secretary had rejected us, not the guru! Next day we peeped inside the gate, hiding our faces from the secretary. When I saw the guru—at the first glance I knew he was not for me. I attended his *satsang* in the second row, and at one moment our eyes met. Such an explosion came in my mind—all the accumulated dirty thoughts burst. I couldn't look at him anymore; he had sent a cleansing current into my little head. Then his face became bigger and bigger, like the sun filled with light. I couldn't look anymore.

At the end of the *satsang* I knew I had experienced some of his

power, but the mind said: No, he is not for you. I took a bus to
Rishikesh, having said bye-bye to that boy and the secretary, the
headache-man.

All my thoughts about yogis and asceticism were finished, but I
had to try again. I spent twenty-four hours in a second-class train—
a bad experience; I was still only nineteen. At last, I bundled myself
into a bus, and in Rishikesh I went to the Sivananda ashram. But
because I had not written a letter, I was not allowed to stay. (Thank
you, I am beginning to expect this, good-bye!) I stayed nearby in
another ashram. Here I saw a lot of nonsense going on; I couldn't get
the Radhasoami teaching out of my head.

I looked at everything under a big light, going from ashram to
ashram, but I rejected everything. I went up in the hills, but I saw,
even with great austerities, yogis are proud, jealous, and not necessarily spiritual at all. All thoughts about asceticism were now finished. But although I wanted to follow the Radhasoamis and couldn't
accept the Beas guru, I did not know that there were other branches
in India with other gurus. It was a puzzlement. What to do? Then I
thought I would continue traveling, looking at gurus, but if I didn't
find anyone better, I would return to Beas.

I don't know how many places I saw: Benares, Allahabad, Lucknow,
Kanpur, Bangalore—all the time asking for enlightened beings. The
final result: they were all negative; they were all talking; they hadn't
gone inside. I became ill with dysentery and malaria, and the doctor
gave me thirteen different pills; I wouldn't touch them. I was so tired
of traveling after six months, I went to lie in the Goa sun. Soon I got
back into meditation. I swam, relaxed, made my own food—had a
holiday. In my heart, there was a seed of *bhakti*; I knew that I had
to give that love to a guru.

But also in my heart, there was much weeping because if my guru
was calling me, why was he giving me such a hard time? Why was
he kicking me around? If I can't find him, I will not live, *bas*—
finished! Then one day I passed a bookshop. I went in; the first book
to catch my eye was *Radhasoami Faith*, a historical study. My mind
was saying: That book is standing there for you; buy it. Without
looking through it, I paid and left. My mind was *blanco*, but I felt
happiness inside. I started reading; first I was puzzled, as I knew the
Beas books were not sold in shops. But it explained itself. Do you
know the book?

Yes, I actually have a copy.

You know it gives the background, the teachings, but most important, all the different splinter groups which I didn't know about. I read it three times. Although it lists so many groups, I knew for the Radhasoamis there can only be one *sant satguru*—the perfect one. This was clearly explained by the author, Agam Prasad Mathur. I accepted everything, but it didn't help me find the correct guru. As everything had started in Agra, I decided I must go there. I must look for my diamond.

After a long journey, I arrived. I prayed: If this city has anything for me, guide me; I'm too tired. The first night was spent in a hotel near this very house. The next day I took a rickshaw to Soamibagh. It is a private colony. I went in with my long hair, looking like a hippy, carrying my rucksack and sitar. In those days, I didn't care what I looked like; that was the outside. Someone came up and said, "This is a sacred place—the place of Soamiji, the place of the Radhasoamis." I told him I knew all that, so he called another man and we talked. He was the eldest son of the fifth guru, Babaji Maharaj, who had departed in 1949. He became critical of Beas when I said I had been there; there are all these groups and all the quarrels about the true succession. When I told him I wanted to stay, he was happy and it was arranged. Foreigners are not usually attracted there.

At 5:00 the next morning, I was wakened to attend *satsang*. People were meditating; the atmosphere was good. There were four life-size paintings of the gurus; I liked the first two, but the others didn't appeal to me. I could accept Soamiji, the first guru, and Hazur Maharaj, the second; the others, no. After two days, I met a man there—an old *satsangi*. His external eyes were blind, but the inner one was open. He could tell if a man was before him or if it was a woman; he could see their astral forms. He said, "You had to come here, but you will not stay—mark my words." He had a large library of Radhasoami books in English, which I went through in two weeks. I was more than ever certain these were the teachings for me.

Did you receive their initiation?

The eldest son gave it, but when he told me for my meditations I was to contemplate on the image of the last guru—his father—I said I would not do that; I could only meditate on Soamiji. From that moment the contact broke; they wanted to get rid of me.

Were you given the full initiation?
Full from their point of view, yes. I am not allowed to reveal the details.

But were you initiated into the sound current?
No. Just the contemplation. That caused enough trouble. I could not accept what they wanted me to do. I went to the *samadh* of Soamiji, bowed my head and prayed for help. Then the strange thing comes: I had found the book *Radhasoami Faith*, but it never occurred to me to meet the author, who was also living in Agra. In Soamibagh, they have been building a great marble *samadh* for the last seventy years; I was given work polishing marble slabs, sitting in the sun, getting four rupees a day. It was the only way I could stay. Thousands come to see the temple, so I too became a tourist attraction.

I spent my nights weeping, praying: You have brought me here, why don't you show yourself? I contemplated suicide. One night when I was half asleep, there was a flash of light and a face I couldn't recognize—very fast. And I was hearing voices, "Why are you worried? Come to me, I will help you!"

I was filled with bliss; who was the man?

Now, another strange thing. In the book *Radhasoami Faith*, there's a picture of the author, Dr. Mathur, and I had read it by that time ten times, yet I never recognized the face. It was still not time to meet him. Three months went by; one day I was buying food. A man came towards me; without thinking, I said, "Please listen to me," and I poured out my whole story to him. He said, "There's only one man who can help you—it's Dr. Mathur." Even then, my mind could not accept that it was the author of that book. Perhaps a shadow was over my consciousness.

We arrived at this very house at 6:00. Dr. Mathur's wife received us. We had tea, we talked, and I was struck by the warmth. After a time, Dr. Mathur came; it was that face! When he spoke, it was that voice! Now the Radhasoami Faith is a hidden faith, and it appeared that Dr. Mathur could not say, "I have called you at last." I also recognized this, so a sort of play went on: "How are you? What is your name?" and so on. Finally he said, "If you want to stay here, I can give you a room." The next day, I received initiation.

The next day? But was it different from the Soamibagh initiation?
There was something new. The initiation that Dadaji gave me—

Dadaji is the name of my guru—meant I could contemplate on the guru I was attracted to; otherwise there was no difference.

Were you given the initiation into the sound current?

That came four months later; I requested it myself. I am convinced my Dadaji is the living *sant satguru* of the Radhasoami Faith. I meditated, served my guru as best I could. This is the path of *bhakti*, so one must serve and attend *satsang* twice daily.

Dadaji gives satsang *twice daily?*

According to his pleasure—sometimes he comes, sometimes not. We know he's always there.

How long is it since you first arrived here at Dadaji's?

Five years. I can say that within six months, I had full understanding of this path.

How much time do you spend in meditation?

A minimum of three hours. At the beginning, I continued with my hatha yoga; I played my sitar, but slowly these things went—a lot of things went. But—as you see—I still smoke.

Dr. Prasad is still teaching at Agra University?

Yes. He follows closely the traditions of the Radhasoami Faith, which puts emphasis on asceticism, but while remaining a householder and having a job. One can also marry and go on with one's sex life. But one must become a vegetarian.

I suppose that means sex life within marriage, and for the means of procreation only?

In this place, one can do as one likes, even go to cinemas and eat in hotels, but be detached. Sitting in the company of the *sant satguru* cleans one. Dadaji never says to leave off sleeping with women; after all, a man must have a sex life. . . .

But when you say a sex life, you mean within marriage?

You are free to have girl friends. The Indian lady who just brought the tea, I have been having for two years. She has been given to me by my guru, but not only to satisfy my sex life—we are all full of lower qualities.

Are you married to that lady?

I am not married, thank you! She very much belongs to me; we are happy together. She has been a *satsangi* for fifteen years. So because she has been given by Dadaji, it's a pure arrangement.

I see. Does Dr. Prasad give initiations regularly?

He never indulges in propaganda; it's prohibited. Why? It is meant only for those fit. If many came through propaganda, most would be unfit.

How does your guru choose who is ready?

The *sant satguru* is charged with the highest spiritual current; he has a direct line with the highest spiritual consciousness; he is the embodiment of that consciousness.

Yes, that is common to the teachings in all branches of this faith; and surely you must know the disciples within each of these branches take their own guru as the sant satguru.

The true *sant satguru* has created ministers with limited spiritual power to serve him—yes, there are the other gurus of this line. Seekers ready come directly here; let's say they are the select souls; others go to the branches. All are growing; we are learning, being cleaned. When we are ready, we get drawn to the right place. This is my realization.

Do you mean the inner realization? Are you in contact with the inner guru in meditation?

Sometimes these things are there—we are not allowed to tell— there are a lot of things.

Well, can you talk about the goal of your sadhana?

First of all, man must realize he is spirit, not the body, mind, or senses. When the body dies, there will be spirit only. It is the illusion of the world that man thinks he is the body. We have to contact the spirit within the body at meditation; that's what the *sant satguru* gives. There are so many layers of consciousness. Without the proper *sant satguru*, you cannot meditate.

But in all branches of Radhasoami the disciples meditate, and I know of some who get very high experiences.

If you go to a third-class shop for a cake, you will get a third-class cake. If you go to a five-star hotel for a cake, you will get something better. Yes, they are getting something. But just look at some of the gurus who have gone to the West with their spiritual tricks. I am asking you, are they not cheap?

It's not my purpose while compiling this book to make such assess-ments. Anyway, I believe everyone is drawn to the guru who is right for him. I am not concerned.

If you have realized, you would be concerned.

Are you saying you are realized?

I have realized they are giving a cheap thing.

As far as I understand it, the goal of the Radhasoami Faith is to become one with the sant satguru—*that is realization. Have you be-come one with your guru?*

That's not an easy thing.

True. How far are you realized?

First a man has to realize he is spirit. . . .

That's self-realization.

The rest is the guru's grace. There's nothing we can do on our own. It's even grace to come here. But we have to work to get grace. In the West, yoga is very cheap. They have made it cheap. They offer instant realization. It is not: it's like walking on a razor's edge. You have to fight the influence of anger, sex, jealousy, ego—thousands of things.

That fight is common to all paths. How far have you been able to conquer these influences since coming here?

What is required is humility. Without that, we cannot get any-where. But our progress is kept hidden. Maybe you are a high soul, but the *sant satguru*, to avoid pride, will keep this hidden from you. You are looking at me—yes, I'm suffering from all sorts of things, but maybe I'm nearly free. The goal of Radhasoami is not a small one: it is *Sat Lok*, the region of pure spirit, the ocean of love, the ocean of bliss.

Can I ask about Dadaji's followers? Does he have any other West-ern disciples?

There are a few.

He has never traveled abroad?

No. He has been invited, but as a historian—he is one of India's eight great historians. An American university requested him, but he will not go. Let me put it very straight: Dadaji is the distributor; the other gurus who have gone to the West are the workers—they are doing the beginning work. Let these people clean up. When they are clean, he will go, *bas!*

Do you have a job here?

My job is to attend *satsang,* and as my *seva,* I write letters to foreigners for Dadaji.

How do you support yourself?

That's a tricky question. For the first year, I lived here without money. Sometimes Dadaji gave me spending money as well as food and clothing. Then the contact with my family grew better, and although I never asked, they send money monthly, which is enough.

Do you see yourself living here for the rest of your life?

I hope so. There's nothing in the West for me. I am trying to get a job in the Dutch Embassy, even as a clerk or gardener. This would enable me to stand on my own legs. And I would like to become an Indian citizen. I know in my past life I was here. I have been called back, *bas!*

· · ·

It is time to catch the night-train to Benares, another sacred city on the Ganges, and an ancient seat of Hindu learning. Arriving there the next day, I head directly for Asighat, the section of the city where many foreigners live.

I have the address of an American girl who spent years here in austere sadhana until she met the son of a government minister, and now they have four children—which has made her popular with her in-laws. She is away, however, in her Delhi house, so there is no interview with her.

I take an interview with a French girl instead, but it doesn't come off well; I can't use it. Then I am shown a hut by the river. It's bleak, dark, sordid . . . Two boys live here, one supposedly taking a Ph.D. at the university. I ask him what he is specializing in. "Resentment!" he answers.

The other boy tells me he is studying in the university of the world. The prospective Ph.D., who is toasting chapatis over an open charcoal fire, grabs the microphone and confirms: "That's the reality, man."

I tell him his chapati is on fire and he thrusts the mike into the flames, saying "Tell your story, man; tell it as it really is!"

His companion informs me that if I want a good interview, I'd better come back at night. "He don't speak until dark." Grateful for this news, I snatch up my things and crawl out into the light. But I have to go back inside to rescue my forgotten blanket. A blond infant is spreading jam over it . . .

I spend the night in a hotel that is cheap and nasty, but at least near the bus stand, from which I leave the next morning for Sarnath, several miles away. In this quiet, sleepy place associated with Lord Buddha, I am hoping to meet some Western Buddhists. But first I go to the Government Tourist Bungalow, which is breathtakingly devoid of life.

Eventually a clerk arrives, his arm in a plaster cast, and shows me to an empty dormitory. The whole place can be mine for six rupees per night, he explains, and the deal is struck. I then go to the Tibetan Institute of Buddhist Studies across the way—the whole of Sarnath is a one-street village, really—but that too is breathtakingly devoid of life. I go up to the library and find it open, but empty, no readers, no librarian. Just one boy reading a Tibetan newspaper. I ask him, where is everyone?

"Sir," he says, standing up, "it's the Dalai Lama: he is this moment arrived at Bodhgaya, and for it all have gone."

Well, yes, all Buddhists—but surely not everyone?

Fortuitously, I find a research scholar (did he miss the train out to Bodhgaya?) who tells me of a young Englishman in a nearby village who works in a leper hospital.

Ah, surely he will have something to say!

But he is incommunicado down a huge well, hammering at an obstinate pump. He yells, "Half a mo—I'll be up soon." The wretched patients are sitting in the sun—the place is more like a home than a hospital; I see that leprosy is not something that everyone can recover from.

From the depths of the well, a smiling face appears. Yes, he will give the interview, but the electric power is off. Perhaps the power-house people have also gone to see the Dalai Lama? No matter, the tape recorder has batteries—and they work.

ANIL BHAI
A hospital for skin diseases
Sarnath
17 January 1981

I hope I'm not interfering with your routine.
I don't spend my life down *there*, if that's what you mean. Anyway, I never get any visitors here, so that will make a change.

What brought you here—can you tell me?
I have been living in the village—Chiraigaon, the village of the birds—for two and a half years. Before that I was in Andra Pradesh; before that I lived in Europe. You see, I was born in England, of Catholic parents—let me see, yes, about thirty years ago—but there I was plain John Davis. Here they call me Anil Bhai—Brother Anil.

I spent six years in a seminary in Birmingham, but in the end, the bishop was not keen to ordain me: he thought I should do more social work. So social work I did, with some Sisters, until I went to Rome and met the Brothers of Charles de Foucauld. I left England with the intention of visiting the Brothers in the desert, but somehow I ended up in Sicily.

Life with the Brothers, and their principles, attracted me very much. I was finally sent to the south of Spain for a year as a formal novitiate; during that time, I did in fact go to the Sahara Desert, where Charles de Foucauld had set up what you could call an ashram. I stayed six weeks. During my novitiate, I was asked by the prior where I would like to go. I replied, "Anywhere outside Europe." I was offered India, so I accepted.

Can you describe what Charles de Foucauld stood for, what he created?

He was born in 1856 of a French aristocratic family. He was thrown out of the army; he left his religion; he explored Morocco (which was then closed—he went disguised as a Jew), and his survey of Morocco is still a standard work, even though his work was hidden. What impressed him was the faith of the Muslims: the adoration of prayer. This brought him back to his own religion. He then joined a silent order, and lived in solitude and recollection. He spent three years in Nazareth, very much the servant—he became the doorkeeper to the Sisters.

He was later ordained a priest in France, but decided to return to the Sahara, where there were no priests. He built a hermitage in Beniabbes. There he stayed many years living a life of silence, although on some days he had perhaps a hundred visitors. His idea was to proclaim the truth not by what we say, but by what we do. He had a big thing about being a brother to all men, and so all the Brothers who follow him carry this on, irrespective of religious differences.

Was he involved in doing good work, social work?

Not really. People came to see him as a brother for advice, for money. He never left his compound—people came to see him. In the Sahara there are only five towns, and there was always trouble with terrorists. In 1916, he was killed in his hermitage: he was alone, without any Brothers. Not until 1932 did six Brothers go to his hermitage to live the life he had lived. Now there are fourteen different Charles de Foucauld families of Brothers and Sisters scattered all over the world. His basic principle was to live amongst the poor—the poorest of the poor. Here in this village we don't find the poorest of the poor, but they're pretty poor.

But what do you actually do here?

We are at the moment three Brothers. The other two are from Goa. Within our fraternity, there's no difference between ordained and non-ordained Brothers. One of the Brothers here works in the village as a carpenter; the other is learning to be a tailor. I am in this leper hospital—sometimes in charge—which I'm not happy about, nor the fact that I have this big room and drive the van. But no one is keen to work in a leper hospital; the patients are maltreated by the doctors as well as society. I am on the medical staff, but as you saw, I also have to fix things like broken pumps. But doing mechanical work keeps me sane.

My main work is going to villages trying to detect early leprosy symptoms, then going regularly to give treatment, doing a little education. On every second Saturday, I go to the main *ghat* in Benares, giving medicines and dressings to the leprosy patients there.

How many patients do you attend to in Benares?

Eighty to one hundred regulars, mostly beggars. It was hard—I can tell you—at first.

Are you given a wage by the hospital?

Three hundred rupees monthly—about $35, I guess. Somehow I manage.

Does your work involve teaching the Gospel?

No, not at all. Charles de Foucauld's basic thing was no teaching, no preaching—we go out of our way to avoid this. We never even accept money from the missions; we want to avoid identification with the Church business. In the village, they all know we are Christians; on Christmas day, lots of people come to see us for *prashad,* and if anyone asks questions, we just answer them. Our aim is to be amongst simple, ordinary, poor people, to treat them as Jesus treated the people of Nazareth.

Have you been influenced by Hindu forms of meditation and prayer?

In a sense, yes; we are affected by the way they pray, by the *arati,* which is unknown in the West, but which we do here. We do not copy, but use the form we are more at home with. We celebrate the Hindu feasts. All the three of us are conscious we are young beginners; so what we are going to be five years from now remains to be seen.

You have chosen a hard way—not only living with the poor, but being poor yourself. Was it difficult to adapt to these conditions?

There are millions living in conditions much worse than these. In the eyes of a Westerner—yes, it's hard, and some people will never adapt. Some Brothers have tried it, and it doesn't work—they can't take it. I have had no problems, partly because I don't worry about what I eat, and if there's nothing to eat, there's nothing to eat. The heat gets bad in summer, well . . . .

Does the electricity ever work?

You can see there's an electric wire that reaches us, and—yes— sometimes it actually works. Last night it came on at 10:00 and went off at 5:00 A.M., which isn't much good to anyone. You can't rely on it.

Can you describe a typical day in your village?

I never have a typical day—all are different. When I come to the hospital in the morning, I never know what is going to happen. We tend to get up at 5:30, wash, go to chapel till 6:30 for silent adoration, then have Mass, read the Psalms and Bible. At 7:30 we cook tea and *roti*; I then shoot off to hospital. Yesterday I was in the city all day long. The day before, I cycled ten kilometers to another village for a clinic; this means I sit by the side of the temple from 8:00 till 10:00, and all sorts of people come. What is important for leprosy patients is regular dressings.

All your work is done in the open?

Oh, yes. Usually with an audience. When the school opens at 10:00, I get all the kids—the foreigner, you know.

How do you sterilize your instruments?

There's none whatsoever. I have to use spirit. I have to work amongst the flies and the muck, and the other day, I had a dead body facing me all the time. I usually get brought lots of cups of tea. When I leave, I have lunch with a neighbor, spend some time on my Hindi studies, return to the hospital—where there's always something to repair—or I might have to take a patient into the city. I'm the only driver. If there are surgery cases, I either bring the doctor here or take the patient to him. In the evening, back in our house, we do the cooking, eat, talk a little, then hit the bed any time between 8:00

and 11:00—it all depends. There are no rules. Once a month we have one complete day off for recollection; I do this away from the house and hospital—just to be alone. The house is usually full of people, mostly village children.

Can you explain the purpose of the two Brothers working here as a carpenter and tailor?

In India you have the *sadhu*, a man consecrated to God, and usually he is supported by the community. We are also consecrated to God, but we follow St. Paul's advice, "Let him who does not work, let him not eat!" Charles de Foucauld was very strong on this because he saw the missionaries sitting about being fed. For us, the key phrase is the hidden life of Jesus of Nazareth. We are living with the poor, but not supported by them.

It's not very obvious being a carpenter or a tailor leading a consecrated life. The clergy in Benares cannot understand what a priest is doing here living as a carpenter or tailor. But this is a calling; it's nothing we've chosen.

. . .

Back in the luxury of my solitary dormitory, feeling suitably guilty, I am writing Father Bede Griffiths; I can fit in a visit to his ashram after Pondicherry. But now I have to send a telegram to the Theosophical Society in Madras, my next port of call. I have just discovered that the journey to Madras will take thirty-six hours, and I may be too late for the wedding of my American friends, Kalidas and Uma.

In India, when we have a lot of time, it's amusing to pay a visit to the village post office; we are often invited in for tea, while the clerk unlocks his cupboards, looking for air-letters. But here I am at the Sarnath post office, tealess, and told it's too inconvenient to send my telegram, could I not go to the main P.O. in Benares?

"Inconvenient . . . ?" I ask, trying not to appear too eccentric. "Very inconvenient," I'm told, "you see, the line, she's out of order!"

I dash all the way to Benares—what else can one do?—and go first to the Indian airline office to beg them for a seat on the afternoon plane. After all, Kalidas and Uma (according to my wife Kate, who is snowed-in at Mussoorie) have arranged their wedding to coincide with my arrival. But there is no chance; twenty-nine people are already on standby for the plane.

In India, there is no queuing system. We all push. And the pushing is especially great in city post offices. I manage to get hold of a telegram form, hand it back, and get hold of a receipt, but I leave the post office all of a heap.

The next morning I am on the train, dazed at the prospect of a thirty-six hour journey. The businessman opposite me in the compartment laughs and tells me the train was twelve hours late last week. I'm resigned by now to missing the wedding, but still hopeful of getting an interview with the couple.

The train is only three hours late, but it is dark, and I'm not even sure if there is a room for me at the Theosophical Society. The businessman lives at Adyar, so we share a taxi, and he helps me get through the locked gates of the T.S. estate. There I find Norma Sastry, the estate secretary to whom I have been writing unsuccessfully— no replies ever reached me.

She looks as if she's been to a party—Oh, a wedding!—and she gives all the news. It was just lovely, and Kalidas and Uma have left only a little while ago for the ashram of—who was it? Norma can't remember, but anyway, I have a room: No. 15 in Leadbeater Chambers. Kalidas has just vacated it.

In the room I find the remnants of a vegetarian party, and on the table a pink telegram:

PILL ARRIVE ONE DAX LATE FULL LOVE MALCOLM

This is a high-style post office creative writing—a free interpretation of my original message:

DUE TO TRAVEL AGENT'S BUNGLING WILL ARRIVE ONE DAY LATE. ALL PLANES TO MADRAS FULL. LOVE MALCOLM.

Madras has three seasons: hot, hotter, hottest. This is only the hot, but in the morning, as I start making arrangements for the first interview, the southern heat is forcing me to walk in the shade of the ancient trees that line the paths of this landscaped estate. It has been the international headquarters of the T.S. for about a century, and there is one resident who still remembers its early days of glory. He arrived as a young man over seventy years ago, and still rides a cycle and speaks in ringing British tones. His mind sparkles in its clarity and consciousness of expression.

I feel a pang of regret—how I wish this interview could be filmed.

*B*efore you speak about your early life, may I ask if it's true that you are ninety-six years old?

No! That's not correct—I'm only ninety-five. Hmm, my early life? Well, I am British, born in London in 1885, June 2. My parents were landed gentry—squires—owners of land and farms. My mother was a low-church Protestant; my father, because of his love of music, would often visit Catholic cathedrals to listen to the music, although he was not a Catholic—he was broad-minded.

I wanted to become an engineer and was accepted at London University for a B.Sc. in engineering, but after one year, I had a six-months' illness with typhoid fever, and another six months to learn to walk again and recover. One little dormouse nurse came to look after me; she had a magnetic power. When I was raving with fever, she would put up her hand and say: "Now Dick, be quiet!"—and I was like a lamb.

When I began to think and recover—and this is the way I came to Theosophy—I said to the little nurse, "Is there nothing more to be known about God and man than what we learn from the parson?" She gave me a strange answer, "There is infinitely more to be known." I said, "Where is it? It's not taught in the Bible." She replied, "It's mentioned in the Bible—Jesus said, 'Unto the multitudes I speak in parables, but unto my own I speak of the mysteries of the Kingdom of Heaven'—that is the further knowledge." Then she told me about the Theosophical Society in London, where I could meet people who had found that wisdom. When I had recovered, I found the Society and went there.

How old were you then?

About nineteen or twenty—it was 1904. There I met Mr. Bertram Keightley, who helped Madame Blavatsky publish her book, *Isis Unveiled*—her first remarkable book, which made the world sit up, prior to founding the T.S. He handed me a form to fill in; there I read the Society's three aims: to form the nucleus of the Universal Brotherhood of Humanity without distinction of race, creed, sex, caste or color; to encourage the study of Comparative Religion, Philosophy and Science; to investigate unexplained laws of Nature and the powers latent in man.

I was in sympathy with these aims and paid the fee. Later I was sent for and met Colonel Olcott—the co-founder of T.S.—who handed me my diploma of membership, shook my hand, and wished me well. He had a powerful, magnetic personality. I then made friends with a staunch Theosophist, Mr. A. P. Sinnett, who claimed to have had contact with the Master Kuthumi—he has written about it in a book called *The Occult World*. Due to his influence, I wanted to become a Buddhist monk and give up Christianity, but he advised me to follow my career for a while. I was still studying T.S. books, but took an apprenticeship on the railways in London, which led to an appointment as assistant engineer of construction in Nairobi for two years. That was a world of candles and kerosene oil.

Did you have any contact there with Theosophists?

No, but I formed a group of three people called the Occult Group. Now I hear there is a live T.S. movement in Nairobi. At night in my tent, I used to read Theosophy. I became more and more interested, and when I returned to England in 1908, I attended lectures by Dr.

Annie Besant, the new President of the Society. I had written to Colonel Olcott about becoming a monk, but he had died, and Dr. Besant replied, "I strongly advise you not to plunge into orthodox Buddhism, but perhaps if we can meet, we can discuss it."

After meeting her three times, she said, "I would like a young man like you to see India. Today I have been given two thousand pounds to do what I like with, so I invite you as my guest at the international headquarters of the T.S. at Adyar." I jumped with joy, but she said, "No, no! Think about it for a week, then let me know." At that time, I was also offered a very good job in West Africa; it meant a high salary and a step up in my career. I was at a crossroads.

Now Mr. D. N. Dunlop was a famous Theosophist who had a miniature of two adepts I recognized as the Masters Morya and Kuthumi; he had copies made for me.

They were paintings?

They were photographs of paintings made in Madame Blavatsky's London studio, I believe; somehow she placed her hand on the painter's head, he saw the Masters, and painted them. I was thrilled to have these copies, and as I was at this crossroads, I placed them before me and sent out a plea: If I am worth being taken notice of by the Society founded at your instigation by H.P.B., could you give me a hint which way to go? I received a definite sentence in my head: Choose the way of unworldly wisdom, and there will be no regrets. It was clear.

I arrived here in 1909, with a letter of introduction from Dr. Besant. I was put in room number seven at Blavatsky Gardens—a very simple room. C. W. Leadbeater had already awakened the kundalini and was cultivating clairvoyance; I went to his Octagonal Bungalow and told the man leading me to say Dr. Besant had sent me. He went in and said, "Dr. Besant has come." I could hear Leadbeater saying inside, "Hmm! She must have materialized; let's go and see." We laughed when we met. And then I met a shy, sorrowful-looking boy—J. Krishnamurthi.

He was about thirteen years old then; I was ten years older. Mr. Leadbeater took me into his confidence when he got to know me better, and said, "Master Kuthumi has asked me and Annie to look after these two children of his." At that time, Krishnaji's younger brother was still alive. I was entrusted with the task of helping. What we had to do was to clean up these two boys: they were unhappy, dirty, ill-fed because their mother had died and a very hard-hearted aunt was in charge of the house. The father was not much good with children, so they were neglected. We set to work.

It was a great joy to me having come into all this. People point to me now and say, "He was Krishnamurthi's teacher." That is not quite true. I was Krishnamurthi's constant companion, his nurse, his *valet de chambre*. We went cycling and swimming together, yes, and I did teach him his first English. I moved with him closely day and night until his nineteenth birthday. That was from the beginning of his career until 1915, when I had to go to war and join the army.

There has been some criticism that the booklet At the Feet of the Master *was never written by Krishnamurthi himself during this period. Do you know anything about this?*

I certainly do. When Mr. Leadbeater first saw the thirteen-year-old Krishnaji, he was struck by his aura, which he described as the most wonderful he had ever seen. It could not have been Krishnaji's outer appearance that was striking, for at that time he was undernourished and uncared for. But Leadbeater took him and his younger brother under his care. The father—who was a Theosophist—and the other children were given a place to live within the Society's grounds. Leadbeater told me Krishnaji was destined to become the World Teacher, "He will undergo spiritual training; there will be opposition, but it has to be done."

Now Mr. Leadbeater had Krishnaji come to him at 5:00 every morning and asked him to recollect what the Master KH had taught him on the astral plane during the night while he was out of the body. I was always present, so I saw Krishnaji write down the teachings in the form of notes. The only outside help he received was in his spelling and punctuation—you see, he was still learning English. But these were the notes that were later turned into the book *At the Feet of the Master* and published under the name of Alcyone; it has been translated into about thirty languages and gone into forty editions or more.

Yes, I know there have been many sceptics who have tried to prove that a boy of thirteen could not write such a book. But I saw him with my own eyes; that is my personal testimony.

That is invaluable testimony, thank you. What happened after you came out of the army?

I became a civilian again in 1924, and Annie Besant suggested I should join Leadbeater in Australia. I was with him for five years, living a strange and wonderful life. I was initiated into Co-Masonry and into other ceremonial groups and helped Leadbeater; I cooked his food and nursed him when he was sick. I toured with him, he made me a priest of the Liberal Catholic Church, and I attended meetings of the esoteric school of Theosophy and the general meetings. A very full life. I plunged into all this with enthusiasm and believed that all I was doing and hearing about were facts.

When you say you believed in everything then, does it mean that later you had doubts?

Well, I'll tell you. I don't doubt, but through the years, because of my strong link with Krishnaji, I seemed to be going through—in a lighter vein, of course—what he went through. So now I have to say that in my book, *The Boyhood of J. Krishnamurthi*, I wrote about things as though I *knew* them, but I had been told them by Leadbeater and others and accepted them as facts. Now I would say that whether they are facts or not I don't know, but because I don't know, I can't deny or affirm.

I see. How did you part with Mr. Leadbeater?

I married. I came back to London. Took a job, but after a time my wife and I came back to Adyar, where we lived, and I was given permission to take a job in a big engineering firm outside.

Was all this before Krishnamurthi renounced his role as the World Teacher?

Long before, oh, yes, yes. . . .

You were still in contact with him in those days?

Yes, of course. I met him often. I met him in Australia and observed the painful fact that Leadbeater, from being affectionately disposed toward him, turned against him and said everything had gone wrong. Krishnaji later told me how he was asked to get out of Adyar and never come back. Well—as everyone knows—he did get out, and it was only a few days ago that, after fifty years, he was invited back by the President of the T.S., Mrs. Radha Burnier, and he walked through these grounds again. I had the pleasure of welcoming him, although

I have been seeing him practically every year when he comes to India. He is now looking in better health than ever. He is eighty-five, you know—ten years younger than me.

All these many years you have lived in India must have been very fulfilling for you.

Yes, they have. I can say this: When I first came to Theosophy, my mind—through contact with the early Theosophists—was filled with visions of the Wise Men of the East, the Great Adept Brotherhood, the Hierarchy standing behind the people who were said to be running the inner government of the world. But all that has rather faded—I don't say it isn't true. Leadbeater wrote a wonderful book about this: *The Masters and the Path.* I have been presented with much teaching and have read many books; I took into my heart what I liked and made it my own. But in the past, I made a mistake—in an effort to help others—by writing and talking about the Masters and what they did and didn't do as if I *knew.* Now whatever progress I have made, I have progressed to this point of view that much of my belief has fallen off me like a cloak: my Co-Masonry, my priesthood, the teaching about karma, reincarnation, and the rest of it. I don't say it isn't true: I say belief isn't knowledge.

But you do follow Krishnaji?

Yes, rather. He looks at us and says, "I suppose I have to talk— why do you come to hear me? Well, the world is in a mess." Then he paints a picture of the chaos of modern life. He asks, "What is the root of chaos?—the power of thought is a great slayer of the real; let the disciple slay the slayer." Krishnaji puts it in his own way and then asks if it's the mind that creates confusion. How to stop the confusion? Well—by realizing it, *that* stops it. Then in freedom from confusion, there's love. That's his message. It's so tremendous, we can't take it.

He's still emphatic that he's not a teacher. I don't touch his feet —I wanted to, I *feel* like it. I told him the other day when I was holding his hand on his historical reentry into this place, "I feel like touching your feet, but I'm not going to." He said, "Quite right!" and laughed.

As a last question, what do you think you have achieved by your seventy-five years' association with the Theosophical Society and Krishnaji?

I am not able to estimate what I have achieved—you or others who meet me may form their own opinion—I can't say I have arrived at this or that. I have learned that nobody can teach me how to meditate—or "muditate," as most people do. And nobody can tell me how to become spiritual or to define God. It's all ineffable wonder and beauty and love. That's what I think; I can't describe it. Should I try, I would destroy it.

. . .

It's just as well that the interview with Mr. Balfour-Clarke was not filmed, for as he spoke the words "And then I met a shy, sorrowful-looking boy—J. Krishnamurthi," a powerful evocation of that moment so many years ago overtook me, and I burst into tears. It was so unexpected that I was helpless for several minutes. Mr. Balfour-Clarke then told me about Mary Luytens's book The Years of Awakening *which gives a truthful account of Krishnaji's tormented early life. He also told me how I could see Krishnaji, for he is still in residence nearby, but outside the T.S. estate.*

Unfortunately, I cannot arrange this meeting as I must soon leave Adyar for Pondicherry, where I will have the opportunity of interviewing another person who was very close to a remarkable spiritual figure. In the meantime, I buy some Theosophical Society books, and look for the letter Kalidas and Uma are supposed to have left for me. I never find it, so I don't know where they have gone, or whether I shall ever catch up with them.

By midday, I am on the bus, and it is still light when I reach Sri Aurobindo Ashram. But the manager of the Cottage Guest House there tells me my letter requesting accommodation never arrived. A few anxious moments pass, but he is able to give me a room—a cool, well-designed, clean, and reasonable room. This, I notice, is one of the ashram's essential characteristics: whatever they do, whatever they make is done and made to perfection.

I am given tickets which will allow me to eat in the communal dining hall. The ashram itself is unlike any other I know of; its buildings are former private homes of much character, dating from French colonial times, and they are spread out over a section of the town— they are actually part of the town. And Pondicherry itself is rather like a North African resort, with palm trees, French street signs, and blue, blue sky.

When Sri Aurobindo was in political trouble with the British during their rule of India, he took asylum here in what was then French-ruled Pondicherry. He never left the place again, yet he drew people from all over India as devotees, and later many came from all parts of the world. One was Mira Richard, who became Sri Aurobindo's alter ego, his link with the outside world, and the builder of his ashram.

Mira Richard became known simply as Mother. Since her passing in 1973, there has been no other physical or spiritual head to run the ashram. The many resident ashramites seem in no need of a living teacher.

One of my interviews is to be with Maggi Lidchi, whose relationship with the Mother was an unusually close, personal one. But first, I meet Dhruva, an American. I share some of my recent adventures with him, and after hearing my one-day-too-soon Agra saga, he makes me repeat it and declares it is nothing less than a miracle. We rush back to my room, as he can manage an interview only before breakfast (he has to go to his work at the hospital)—which means we shall both be able to indulge in something more nourishing than food.

*C an you start by telling me the meaning of your name and then
how you were drawn into this new life?*

Dhruva is the name the Mother gave me in 1970. She gave the
words "Firm, Fixed, Resolute"—they were translated into Dhruva.
It's also the name of the polestar, the symbol of constancy. Mother
usually named people in terms of the qualities needing to be developed, you see.

Well, I was born in Massachusetts but was brought up in California.
Under quiet protest, I went to school and managed to get a B.A. in
anthropology, more or less by accident. For a while I had a literary
theater in San Francisco and lost a pile of money. When that was
closing down, I met a fellow involved in the esoteric, mainly Egyptian
geometry and mathematics. He was on his way to India to find his
guru, but about the time he arrived in Pondicherry (without me

knowing what he was doing) I found a book of Sri Aurobindo. Later, when I arrived here, that connection developed.

I first wrote to the Mother in 1966, and that was the beginning of the confirmation from her that there was an inner receptivity which might be developed. I came, and here you find me—the therapeutic work I'm doing began here.

I see. Can you describe this work?

It's mainly the alternate modalities of acupuncture and osteopathy, and some homeopathy. I work at one of the ashram clinics. There's one main dispensary and also a surgical clinic and nursing home which I work in.

Is this run on a voluntary basis or do people have to pay for treatment?

A mixture. At the main dispensary, anyone living as a member of the ashram or Auroville can get free treatment. If they want to put something in the box, that's all right. It's supported by ashram funds. In the clinic where I'm working, anyone can come for treatment and pay normal fees, though ashram residents are treated free, of course.

What was it like meeting the Mother?

I met her on the day of my arrival—8 February 1968. I had never been out of the United States before. The plane was late, India was overwhelming, and the scheduled meeting was two or three hours late. The room was full of people, and at that time there was no great revelatory experience, partly because it was early in my inner development, and partly because of the sensory overload of just being in India. There were later experiences, but the most dramatic in its impact was—I think it was New Year's Day 1971. Mother had been extremely ill and hadn't been seeing anyone; she was over ninety then! At Christmas she had had biscuits distributed with a card saying "Persevere." But on New Year's Day, she allowed the heads of the departments to see her; afterwards she said, "Maybe I'll see a few more people." She ended up seeing six hundred! I was at the tail-end of the procession, so when someone called me, I literally ran up the stairs. I was unprepared and therefore more open. That was a very powerful time.

Had Mother been associated with Sri Aurobindo from the beginning of his mission?

He came to Pondicherry in 1910, after a period in jail in Calcutta for his political activities. In jail he had certain inner experiences which gave him the opening to the possibility of this yoga, and from then he was engaged in intense *sadhana*. The Mother, who was French, came here in 1914 with her then-husband, Paul Richard. She later said that she had never surrendered to any entity other than the idea of the Divine. When she met Sri Aurobindo, she immediately, without question, gave everything. She made the extraordinary statement that if that was a mistake, it was the mistake of the whole being.

When the First World War came, she went back to France. She later spent several years in Japan, but returned to Sri Aurobindo and Pondicherry in 1920. Until her death fifty-three years later, she never left. In 1926, Sri Aurobindo had an experience which was described as Krishna coming into the cells of his body; after this—for twenty-four years, that's until his passing—he never went outside his room. From that day in 1926 the ashram came into existence; through the Mother, the building-up of the ashram and the selecting of those destined to live and work in it took place.

What is the nature of the yoga and sadhana *which has evolved?*

One of the difficulties about talking about it is that it can only come through one's own understanding, which is limited, and one is in danger of speaking in platitudes and jargon. Well, let's try. Sri Aurobindo came to spirituality through an intense love for India; he wanted power to free India, so he took to yoga. Then all these other things started happening.

Basically he says that each of the traditional yogas take up one aspect of the human experience: *hatha* yoga deals with the purification and suppleness of the body to make it an instrument to receive; in *bhakti* yoga, the heart is opened; in *jnana* yoga, the mind; in *tantric* yoga, the experiences of occult power and unity, and so on. Each of these paths is a kind of linear opening through a particular faculty in the human makeup, the theory being that as the Divine is everywhere, it doesn't matter *where* you touch it—as long as you touch it. Once that is done, the work is done.

But Sri Aurobindo felt that wasn't sufficient, as each yoga—and religion—represents in its essence a surrender of that part to the Divine, whereas essentially the totality of the human experience has to be surrendered. It became clear to him that the symbol—you can call it the reality—through which that surrender is made is the Divine Shakti, the Divine Mother. He became so identified with that quality of divinity that for some time he signed his name "Kali." He felt the surrender of the total being was the preparation of the body for a greater role to play in the higher scheme. This surrender could bring into the earth's atmosphere a consciousness which up till now has been attainable only by leaving the earth plane in *samadhi*.

This plane of consciousness he refers to as the Supermind. But there's also the Overmind, which as I understand it is the plane of the gods. This [the Overmind] is limited by what we might call the seed (though not the actual outgrowth) of ignorance, because the gods—the power of knowledge, the power of action, the power of love, and so on—function as separate entities. In the Supermind, you have all the multiplicity, the action of diversity, which never loses touch with the One, the Divine. His idea was that if that Supramental force—he referred to it as the Truth-consciousness—could come into the earth's atmosphere and be active instead of implicit, there could be a major evolutionary change in the human makeup. That is what he was working on from 1926.

What was his method of sadhana *to achieve this?*
He said surrender to the Mother was the only effective method.

Do you mean the Mother Kali or the living Mother?
The Mother who came here, the French lady—she was the embodiment of the Divine Mother. So for those doing his *sadhana*, the surrender to her symbolically and in physical fact is the ultimate symbol which enables a far deeper thing to happen than just doing what she may say at a particular moment. Somebody asked Sri Aurobindo in the early thirties, "Did your 1926 experience enable you to realize that Mother was the Divine Mother?" He said he knew much earlier.

Many times he was told, "It's all well and good for you to do this great *sadhana*, but you are you and we are just people." But he would answer, "Look, if my being here has any meaning, it's only in that it enables others to do what I've done."

So the central technique of his yoga is surrender?
Surrender, devotion and love for the Mother is the motivation, and

through that, one contacts the Lord. Sri Aurobindo speaks of the Psychic Being—which is almost the same thing as the soul: it's the evolving entity behind the different parts of us, and it's that which reincarnates.

Recently, I read a summary of Carl Jung's psychology called *The Symbolic Quest*, by Edward Whitmont. I had wondered for a long time what it was in Jung's psychology, profound as it is, that makes it second best to Aurobindo's. Whitmont, in analyzing Jung's approach to the ego and self, makes it clear: we have made the mistake of identifying individuality with the ego, and the self with the Divinity, which makes a fundamental duality in our perception. The ego is formed through the body symbolism—the body image. So in India we have "I am not the body; I am not this; I am not that," in the course of which the true individuality is sacrificed.

In the West, we make the opposite mistake: to avoid losing the individuality, we absorb our self into the physical consciousness—the ego consciousness. Through the same error in perception, both ways have made the opposite end of the mistake: India sacrificing the individual to revel in the Divine, the West sacrificing the reveling in the Divine to sustain the individuality.

For me, Sri Aurobindo's experience—his perception—of the third entity, the Psychic Being, the true individuality that doesn't lose its touch with the Divine, is all-important. In Jungian psychology, there's the constant battle of the ego and the self, the ego having to defend itself all the time because it knows all the cards are ultimately in the self's hand, and the self gradually imposing itself on the ego structure so that the sense of individuality is in jeopardy at each step. In opening the Psychic Center, which Sri Aurobindo says is behind the heart, that problem doesn't exist, as this Center is the link to our true individuality; its essential qualities are quietness, delicacy, joy in giving, and a gentle assertiveness. The awakening of the Psychic Being obviates the dualistic struggle. Sri Aurobindo's suggestion is also that we don't have to dump the body—of evolutionary necessity, we shouldn't do it.

In this yoga, is there a form of initiation and ethical rules, or a special meditation technique?

The general answer to all that is "No." In my case, perhaps an initiation took place when I first wrote to Mother saying I had a problem of being lonely—to which she replied, "Those lonely in the world are ready for union with the Divine." This was the confirmation that something could happen. The ashram is basically vegetarian, but there's no rule about that; it's just felt there are better ways to be nourished than by eating meat. The Mother didn't want a lot of rules because of the variety of ways people get to where they are going.

There are, however, four ashram rules: no sex, no politics, no smoking, no drinking. When the drug thing happened, that was included in the "no smoking and drinking." The "no politics" rule was once explained by Mother in a tape-recorded talk: After Sri Aurobindo came here, he never again engaged in politics, not because he wasn't interested in what was going on in the world, but because in order to be a successful politician, you have to develop hypocrisy, deceit, and so on, which goes against the grain of spiritual development.

Now the sexual question—which is an extremely important one, for the body as it has evolved is made to produce more bodies—is a fairly substantial limitation on many people's behavior. In this restriction, Sri Aurobindo said he didn't mean only the physical act but the vital exchange that can occur between a man and woman without physical contact. It's a technical problem in the *sadhana*, not a moral one. One is trying to do something else with the energy; the sexual energy is the energy of change which, if used in the ordinary way, drains away the chance of the ultimate change—the settling in of the higher consciousness. This cannot be attained if the energy flows outwards, sexually.

How does this affect married couples here?
Sometimes disastrously, sometimes it changes the relationship to a higher, better level, usually something in between. Sri Aurobindo himself said it is one of the most difficult areas in the *sadhana*. Another writer said: Traditionally, by rejecting sexuality, the yogi rejected a whole aspect of physical existence, but this was valid if that rejection ensured a higher body-consciousness, for the energy continues to have a role; it functions in the *sadhana*.

You have given such a vivid outline of the teachings, could you now describe how it affects your daily life?
I can do that in a general way; personal details may be interesting, but not the crux of the matter. I should say that it wasn't until I came here that I had any real life, any focus. I knew there was something

I was supposed to be doing, but I certainly wasn't finding it where I was. The only real sustenance which kept me together was music, mainly Bach, from the time I was sixteen. You were a musician; you will understand all that. Mother says somewhere that it takes a large proportion of one's *sadhana* to simply cancel out the early influences, the lack of clarity, the subconscious habits, all of which are far more powerful than we like to admit. So to get one's past into some kind of creative perspective is a major part of our work.

All I could manage of that first book by Sri Aurobindo was the introduction—about forty pages. And when that fellow wrote saying he was in Pondicherry, it seemed natural: The Mother is there; off we go! Psychologically, my past was the leverage that made this yoga a natural thing to do, although some may say it's a form of compensation. In the beginning this may be a psychological mechanism working as a hook, but later Mother forces you to drop it. It may get you in, but once in, it will be obvious the psychological compensatory stuff has to go.

I didn't know what I would do here in terms of work, but as soon as the possibility of going into healing work came up, that developed naturally; so that problem was solved. There's a fundamental change, and when that happens, one realizes that everything else was a preparation. I was once describing my one drop of understanding of these issues. I said: Is it so difficult to understand that everything is the Divine? And as I said that, I experienced a tremendous . . . blop! And it was so strong, I was completely out of contact: I had to say to myself, I'm not ready for this—if I do this now, they will take me off to the loony bin!

When you say "not ready," what do you mean?
The experience of the Divine being in everything, in every tiny bit of existence. Those experiences come and go, but it takes years to develop some stable capacity to bear a consciousness which is— how to say?—well, which is not natural to the human frame. Let's put it that way. When people asked the Mother, "How do we know when that thing's happened?" she would answer, "You know!—If you have to ask the question, it hasn't happened."

The only preparation is the aspiration to change, to surrender. We try to change the very fiber of what makes us normally human, which happens to be a great deal more normally animal than we like to admit. If there weren't that fundamental idea of giving every single moment as an offering, the thing would be impossible—there wouldn't be a focus.

I saw on the notice board that tonight there would be a recorded performance of Mozart's Requiem. *Do you still listen to music?*

Oh, yes. The ashram provides a wide variety of possibilities of expression. You can paint or dance or play basketball. There's Western and Indian recorded music. There's meditation. But no one says: This is what you have to do!

There's no fixed daily program?

No. You probably know there's also quite a lot of small-size businesses associated with the ashram, mostly handicrafts. Early on, Sri Aurobindo and Mother had to decide whether they were going to do this *sadhana* for themselves as a point of leverage for the rest of humanity, or to include people in the process. They decided to include people; so symbolically, they had to have the whole of humanity here, at all stages of spiritual awareness, from zero to those "highly" evolved. That's why there are outlets for everyone. There are in fact about two thousand people living here permanently—Indian and non-Indian.

Is there a reason why Mother didn't appoint a spiritual successor to carry on the spiritual work?

When Sri Aurobindo left, she was there, so it was assumed she would continue his work. Now there is a problem, because a number of people here implicitly or explicitly have set themselves up as gurus. But this yoga hasn't been finished yet; so you can't be a guru unless the *sadhana* has been finished—even Sri Aurobindo and Mother never finished the process. They just said, "If you want to come along with us, this is what you have to do, this is what's been done so far." Sri Krishna never left a successor. Here it's not thought that the Mother has left with her physical passing; her consciousness is experienceable with a little bit of openness. It's very real.

. . .

In a walled-in garden with bougainvillea falling all over the place and many potted plants, are two white wrought-iron chairs. I am sitting in one of them, waiting for Maggi Lidchi. She comes out of the house with a glass of lemon-water for me—so thoughtful, for it's very hot.

Before she starts her interview, she says she would feel more comfortable if I told her something about myself. Only fair. . . . I give her a five-minute summary of highlights from my strange life, to which she listens attentively—she is such a sweet person—and even asks the most charming questions. But wait, perhaps she is trying to put off her interview? Perhaps she is too polite to say no?

Perhaps. She suggests a walk around the garden. Or—would I like another drink? But now she is actually telling me about her childhood. She speaks English with a Kensingtonian accent, but as she talks, her speech becomes slower and slower. When I ask about her relationship with Mother, she breaks down in tears. After some time she says "I'm so sorry; it's just a bit painful. If you come back tomorrow I'll try again. . . . I'm sure you understand."

I do. I also had a close relationship with my own guru, and he too is no longer on this earth plane.

The next day, Maggi is even more tearful; the interview cannot be finished. But on the morning before I leave Pondicherry, it falls into place. Afterwards, Maggi doesn't feel she has done justice to her relationship with Mother, but still, it's a remarkable testimony, even in its understatement; I feel a little of Mother's fragrance comes through.

MAGGI LIDCHI
Sri Aurobindo Ashran
Pondicherry
23, 24, and 25 January 1981

I was born in Paris. When I was seventeen, I found a French translation of Sri Aurobindo's *Essays on the Gita*. I bought it, not knowing why. Something attracted me to it. I read the essays for two years. And I can say without undue modesty that I understood them not at all. But I was compelled to continue reading them. One day, something opened, and they became clear—they must have been absorbed somewhere in me.

Something then happened which was so important for me that I didn't immediately grasp that these essays had been written by a living person. At the time, Sri Aurobindo was still alive, so technically I suppose I could have taken a plane and come to India. It never occurred to me to write to the publisher.

I did, however, go on looking for other books by Sri Aurobindo; I found *The Synthesis of Yoga*—only the first volume had come out. I read it to the exclusion of everything else for several years. Finally, when I found out the author had started an ashram in India, I also found out that he had just left the body.

This must have been in the early fifties.

Exactly. In any case, I wanted to come to the ashram, for I knew if there was a teaching for me anywhere, this was it. It looked as if it would be difficult to get to India—I was married, living in South Africa. Someone urged me to write to the Mother; I explained I had long wished to come to the ashram, but it seemed impossible. A reply arrived a few weeks later—my first from India. I was excited, but it just said when the time came I would certainly come to the ashram. I thought: That's nice and encouraging—but I couldn't see much chance.

Not long after, I had to leave Africa—I was living in Mozambique—to look after my dying mother. This made me realize that if I could leave for six months, it was perhaps possible to also go to India. In 1959 it did happen; I had to come a roundabout way and not startle my family too much. Through Manila for a UNESCO conference, then Japan, which was all right too, then India, which was my true destination.

You came straight to the ashram?

Oh, yes—it was a pilgrimage, although I wasn't sure what would happen. I came to the *samadhi* of Sri Aurobindo, and something did happen. I knew I had done the right thing. But there were things in the ashram—the Indian form of devotion—which I wasn't prepared for, things which can be startling to the Western mind. I associated this with the Mother rather than Sri Aurobindo. I wasn't too happy seeing photos of Mother's feet stuck up everywhere. And when I was offered photos of Mother which had been blessed by her, something in me withdrew and I became upset. It seemed to me if the ashram Sri Aurobindo had founded wasn't working, where else in the world could one go?

Someone who knew about this turmoil going on in my mind suggested I ask Mother for an interview, she being entirely responsible for running the ashram. Well, when I saw her, all reservations fled; in fact, when I looked into Mother's eyes, everything resolved and tears began pouring down my cheeks. Nothing else mattered—nothing mattered at all. Then I realized something I had read in Sri

Aurobindo's books, but had never taken in: her consciousness was the same as his, though it manifested differently.

When I understood that, I didn't mind what was going on in the ashram—it was irrelevant to the fundamental thing I had come for. That consciousness touched me, so I never again worried about the things that had first worried me. I went back home to put my things in order, then returned to stay for good.

Does that mean you had the approval of your family?
No. My husband realized once I came here it would be the end of our marriage. My mother had died, but I can't say my father and brother regarded it favorably, yet when they saw I was happy here, after some years they gave their blessings.

What did you have in mind once you decided to stay? Did you wish to meditate, do seva, or get into the crafts?
It was entirely yoga. When I was in Africa, I was meditating for at least six hours a day, and I read for another three hours. The moment I got here, everything stopped. I didn't want to meditate, and soon I stopped reading. There was a part of me that hadn't settled down in India—to ashram life—and found itself jammed-in and went on strike. It was difficult. Obviously, the major part of me—the soul —had chosen to be here, and it wasn't going to be at peace anywhere else. But something else would say: No!—and block complete integration.

I started thinking: That is the end of my yoga for this life; I just have to sit it out. This went on for two years, and my health was affected by the conflict. The heat didn't make it any better, but I have since found one can live with the heat if all else goes well. I had such constant dysentery that I had to leave for a while—my father sent me an air ticket. But when I was out, and in spite of the lovely climate, I wanted to get back.

Did it take long for you to be able to return?
Only two months—I never meant to stay away. But suddenly, everything became unblocked. Then I suppose I had the decisive experience of my life by yoga.

It was an inner awakening?
Yes.

Can you speak about your relationship with Mother?

Well—it was rather close. . . . That's most difficult, rather personal, you see. . . .

Did she give you any form of initiation?

People were touched by her and recognized her as their guru—yes, there was an outer form.

She gave a mantra?

Yes, in fact, but one can only speak personally. She gave me a mantra without my asking. But if people asked for one, she would give one. It wasn't like in other ashrams where once they accept a disciple, a form of initiation is automatically given. The mantra she gave me was in French; I haven't seen it anywhere else—but it was given for a special reason.

Mother didn't lay much stress on doing meditation?

In the years I was in contact with her, in speaking to her, and through reading disciples' letters to her in which they asked for meditation instructions, she didn't encourage it much, no. She used to say, "I never had time for meditation, and what I understand true meditation to be is when something takes you by the scruff of the neck and compels you to meditate; to sit down and expect the mind to be quiet is often fruitless and you would do better to read Sri Aurobindo."

You must have spent much time helping her with letters.

Yes, indeed. Everybody would write—there were hundreds of us, thousands! From little children to—well, everybody. You see, she wasn't seeing people toward the end; most people only saw her once a year on her birthday. So people wrote to her, and that was the main form of contact other than inner contact. She was running the ashram at a practical level also. I wasn't the only person reading the letters to her, though. There was a time when she was available three times a day, but when I came she had stopped going out or playing tennis, which she loved.

Can you describe your life here now?

I teach at "Knowledge"—our center of education—what is called the higher course. This year it is on Creative Writing, although the first word is redundant to me.

Are these courses open to everyone?

No, just for our students. We believe in small classes; they are aged about seventeen to eighteen, and are mostly Indian. For several years I did courses on mythology, legends, and fairy tales. And I once taught the younger children science and English.

How long have you actually been residing in the ashram?

It's been twenty years now.

But how do you spend most of your day? Can you say?

I give this course at Knowledge in the mornings at 7:45. I have no set meditation times. Sometimes I go to the ashram before I start the day's activities. When I come back, I write. Of course, when Mother was here, I used to do other work for her: there were translations from French into English. Until recently, I worked on the centenary edition of her work. But now, apart from the teaching, the time is my own. I am involved to a certain extent with a home for little abandoned children.

This house you are living in, is it part of the ashram property?

It is. It used to be the stables of the house next door, in French Colonial times—of course, we have built on to it. I love these walled-in gardens.

Could you share anything personal that Mother would tell her followers? You must have heard so much.

What can one say? Something that she must have said to ten thousand others, but every time I was with her—reading the letters, putting down the answers as she dictated them—her advice was the same, "Surrender to the Divine!—Surrender!" Perhaps through this constant contact with her, one was able to give oneself up to the Divine Will—to offer oneself to the Divine Will. It's the only way to solve anything. I suppose this was her greatest gift; so what she said about surrender is what has stayed on with me. The decisive experience in my yoga is centered around this: One simply says Yes to everything that happens to one.

I was touched the other day by a retarded child in Italy who for the first time has begun to realize she is different; her parents took her to a priest, and he gave her a prayer-like mantra—very simple: "Si, Signor, si, Signor." Acceptance. One always must say "Si." One never says "No"—unless one is crazy. If the Divine has any interest in you, He will see that you don't say No. He will put enough pressure on you to make you understand.

Here's something personal. One day, Mother asked me if I prayed. In fact, since that decisive day I don't, because if you are saying "Si, Signor," you know everything is being looked after, and you trust that as you don't know what the right thing is, it's rather a waste of time praying for anything. So now, if I am hard-pressed, the only prayer is: Let whatever I do be according to Thy Will. This was the reply I gave Mother. She said, "That's very good. . . . There's just one word lacking to make it perfect—add: spontaneously!"

That was Mother's message finally. There's no longer any effort in anything one does once we don't have to bend our will to it. Mother often said, "For those offering to go through the transformation, they must be prepared to go through whatever they have to go through." Then she would add, "But be happy, be joyful!"

This is how she spoke to her followers?

You know, she hardly ever spoke—she gave silent *darshans*. One of the beautiful things in my memory of my time with Mother was watching people's reactions to her. Quite often, I would be asked to arrange an interview for somebody. . . . So many could come, it was difficult at times. I remember one person who spoke non-stop, often critically; you must know about intellectuals barging into ashrams and what a pain they can be. For two days, right until the moment she went up to see Mother, this woman never stopped talking—quite amusing but snide remarks about devotees and aspects of ashram life which to outsiders *can* be regarded as ridiculous.

We went up at last; we saw Mother. Mother didn't say anything. They just looked into each others' eyes, and she was struck dumb. She left thirty-six hours later, without saying anything. She just sent me a note, "I finally realized why I had to come to the ashram."

That often happened. One would take in a strutting, arrogant person, and he would come out melted, weeping copiously, not knowing where the door was. One had to edge them out gently by the elbow, to prevent them going out through a window. They would then sometimes sit on the steps weeping helplessly, not being able to say why. It was as if the true being of the person swam up to the surface when they saw Mother. She was so kind: she would give people flowers whenever they came to see her.

What was Mother's room like?

It was like walking into a different world; it was like being suspended halfway between heaven and earth—because of her presence. The room was always full of flowers, and a sort of spiritual fragrance. The light was incredible. Then there were the French perfumes she wore. All this is not easy to describe; you must know what it's like to be in your own guru's presence.

When I left you the other day, I commented on the marked physical resemblance you have to Mother. Did she ever mention this?

When I first came to the ashram, Mother asked me where I was from. I told her I was born in Paris but I didn't have any French blood, as I was of Spanish-Jewish descent, my father having been born in Turkey. She said, "Oh, Maggi, just like me!" Then I told her that half my family were from Turkey, the other half from Egypt. She said again, "Oh, Maggi, just like me!" We went into whether we should speak together in English or French—she was also born in Paris. But when I told her I had learned my French from an English governess and that I spoke it with an English accent, she again burst out, "Oh, Maggi, just like me!" Well, I am telling you this, but it was one of those little things.

A final question. Could you say something about your writing? I was told your second novel is about to be published in London.

I write. Just novels. I'm working on the third now, which Gollancz is interested in—they published the others. Obviously, if you live in an ashram for twenty years, something of that life creeps into your writing. I enjoy writing enormously; I think it's because the mind goes quiet. I'm lucky, in that one is allowed to express this freely here. There are so many ways of enjoying spiritual life. The great thing is joy. We are not ascetics here, you see.

· · ·

Two minutes away from the main ashram, there are all sorts of boutiques, show places for the many ashram handicrafts and hand-made clothes. I must look for cooler clothes—I'm feeling oppressed by this winter heat. Everything I see is elegantly finished, and after years of wearing Indian khadi (rough, handwoven material), I can't see myself going back to this. But along the main street, I see a

Gandhi homespun shop; there I can buy a kurta pajama: cool, un-pretentious, and in any ashram, you can feel at home wearing them. My last night in Pondicherry is spent with Dhruva. We have dinner—something rare for me, as we don't eat in Mussoorie after tea-time—and listen to his recording of Mother's voice. Then we listen to music, and I am thinking about Mozart and Bach and how their utterances are as sacred and timeless as those of the saints.

The next morning I make too much allowance for catching the bus to Tiruchirapalli (I'm an hour too soon). At 7:00 we are off, and I find that my new, cool clothing is a blessing, for the bus is a local stop-everywhere contraption. When traveling in India, we do not carry books or magazines to read: we are expected to talk to everyone. You have to ask a lot of questions. You have to answer a lot of questions: Where is your wife, how many children do you have, why not?

By four o'clock, after many bumps, many stops, and many questions, I arrive at Shantivanum—hot, tired, speechless. Saccidananda Ashram is off the main road, set in a maze of fields and banana trees hugging the banks of the River Cavery. It is described as a unique prayer center, where people of different religious traditions meet to grow together in the unity which is implicit in all religions. Everything here is rustic and basic and free from concrete decoration. Perhaps all ashrams start life this way. . . .

Father Bede Griffiths—whose books The Golden String *and* Return to the Center *present a synthesis between Hinduism and Christianity—is coming to greet me; I am surprised to see he is wearing pale ocher sadhu clothes. He tells me I am in time for his lecture on the* Upanishads, *and then, very practically, points out that if I am to reach my tomorrow's destination before dark, I will have to take the early morning bus (again). "So we had better have the interview after my talk—will that suit you?"*

An hour later he is leading me to his hut: a bed, a table, two chairs, an unpainted cupboard made out of a packing case (stenciled instructions are still visible—"handle with care"). He is concerned about my comfort as he knows I have been traveling since daybreak. He offers me the best chair.

C ould I start, Father, by asking how you came to embrace Hindu philosophy and religion?

First I came to Christianity, then to Catholicism, then after a short transition, to a Benedictine monastery in Gloucester, England. There I was professed as a monk and there I was ordained a priest. When I was still seeking, I read the *Bhagavad Gita*, then the *Dhammapada*, and books like that. This interest in Indian thought revived when I met a remarkable woman in London—Toni Sussman. She'd been one of Jung's first disciples; she was a psychologist and had studied yoga under a Hindu yogi in Berlin. She was German by birth. She had many books on Oriental thought, yoga, and Vedanta, and this opened a new world for me.

When was all that happening, and how old were you?

It was in the '40s, and I must have been in my thirties. . . . yes, I'm over seventy now.

What actually brought you to India?

This is my twenty-sixth year here, and I came through an Indian Benedictine monk to start a monastery in India. After some difficulty, I got permission to join him. We started a small ashram-monastery in Bangalore; it didn't work, for various reasons. I then met another monk, so together we started an ashram in Kerala. We lived in Indian style and studied Indian scriptures, but the ashram was still Christian in its setup.

In 1968, I moved on to this ashram, which has an interesting history. They had the vision of Christian life lived totally in the context of Indian life and thought. That was their plan. Father Monshanin was a holy man and scholar, but he only lived another seven years; he left before anything was accomplished. His companion, Father la Saux, took the name Abhishiktananda, but after some time went to live in the Himalayas. He completed a whole series of wonderful books—they are getting rather well-known now: a book on prayer, one called *Saccidanand* . . . (a masterly book); and *Hindu-Christian Meeting Point*. The idea is to find a meeting point in the cave of the heart—how the two traditions can meet in the inner heart, the center of the being. In 1968, he invited us to take over this ashram, so we have been gradually building it up and trying to follow this path of Christian life and prayer into the context of Indian life, Indian spirituality.

From the attendance at your talk, I could see the majority were Westerners. Does this mean the meeting point of the two traditions is not so attractive to Hindus?

Many do come from the West, but in recent years, more and more are coming from India. In fact, fourteen Sisters from a religious congregation were here for ten days. The Church in India is very Western, but gradually is discovering its Indian traditions. In the holidays, we have more Indians than Westerners.

Can you explain, Father, the significance of your wearing the orange robe?

Yes—that was a definite choice. You see, we were monks in England, and we feel the same as *sannyasis* in India—both have fundamentally renounced to seek God. In India the ocher robe is the sign of *sannyas*, renunciation. We feel this signifies our life; it is the sacred color—it has a meaning in India, whereas our Western dress has no meaning.

How is all this taken by the Church authorities?

We have been fortunate; we have had the support of the bishops. And since the Vatican Council, this understanding—they call it "enculturation," Christian life should be enculturated, should adopt the culture of the country—is now accepted everywhere. So on the whole, we get good support.

When I was entering the meditation hall, I saw a sign saying there is no entry unless one is initiated. Can you explain what this means?

Yes . . . that is rather particular. One of the Brothers here gives courses in meditation—usually five or ten days—and he doesn't like people wandering in. People should take the whole course and be initiated into his method of meditation. Normally everybody is welcome.

Does that mean the Brothers take on disciples and are regarded as gurus as in the Indian tradition?

Yes, this Brother in particular. He comes from a traditional Catholic family, but since he came here he has learned yoga and is now a master of yoga. He has written a good book, *Yoga and Contemplation*; he has developed a method of yogic meditation using the Prayer of Jesus in the Eastern Church as the base. He has disciples from here and abroad.

Father, during your talk you spoke of the positive aspect of incidents which are usually regarded as disasters. You also gave an interesting interpretation of maya. *Could you repeat the basic points?*

In one of the *Upanishads*, it says that *maya* is the thing made, and the Lord is the *mayin*, the maker. I explained it comes from the root *ma*, to measure. So *maya* is literally that which is measured—the created world, really—and the Lord is the creator. *Maya* means "illusion" in the sense that when people mistake the created thing for the reality—and don't realize it comes from the Creator—they create an illusion that this world is real and Brahman is unreal, whereas *Brahman* is real and this work a manifestation, a form of Brahman.

As the whole world comes from God-Brahman, he is present in every particle of matter, in every living thing, in every human situation. But we judge things from a limited point of view, so sometimes it seems to us this is an accident, this is a disaster. If we could see everything in the light of Brahman, the Eternal Reality, we would see *everything* has a positive meaning. The art of life is to see that which appears to be bad or evil as in fact something positive working. This understanding can bring a transformation in one's life.

Is this approach taught in the Christian tradition also?

Yes, I would say so. What has come to me gradually is the belief that the Hindu tradition—in the *Upanishads* and *Bhagavat Gita* particularly—is fundamentally the same as the Christian tradition. There are different ways of expression, but behind it all I discern the same fundamental doctrine. I also explained that some think Hinduism pantheistic, some monistic, and some polytheistic. All those elements *are* present. But if you go deep enough, you discover something beyond that, which I express in the terms Total Immanence and Total Transcendence. That is both Christian and Hindu.

Another point was your interpretation of the Hindu rite attached to taking food.

In the Hindu tradition, every action should be a sacrifice. Sacrifice is the center of the universe; everything comes from above, we receive it, and it has to return. That is called turning the wheel of the law, the *dharma chakra*. Sin is when we appropriate something and say we can do what we like. This is how we separate ourselves from the cosmic order. Sacrifice preserves the cosmic order.

That concept should be present in everything: when we build a house, undertake a journey, take a bath, eat food—we always relate to the Transcendent Reality. That's why I explained that normally a devout Hindu has his food served on a banana leaf—it's very simple, very beautiful—then he pours water round it and purifies the space. Then the food is offered to God, eaten, and in consuming it, it's burned in the fire within, making it an offering to God. So every meal should be a conscious sacrifice: we receive it, and return it.

In all the years you have lived in India, Father, you must have seen many Westerners looking for a way out of darkness.

Yes, we certainly get a great many here. Most are in search—very seriously, I think. Many have Christian backgrounds, but have been to ashrams. I have seen people who have not been to Mass or practiced any religion for years. But they are seeking God; they are seeking for God within a Christian context—quite spontaneously, they come back to it.

There was a remarkable example of a young man from Brazil, brought up a Catholic. He never went to church; none of his friends did either. His father was an important man in Brazil. He dropped out, wandered through Europe, joined a Hindu sect, came to India, joined a Christian group, and found that book on prayer by Abhishiktananda. He came here and stayed for six months, living in extreme simplicity in a mud hut, wearing a *dhoti*, meditating and reading the scriptures. He became converted. Most interesting.

That is somewhat exceptional, but some find their way like that. Certainly those we get here, even though they don't become Christian, are still really searching and are being led. Something is leading them toward understanding.

Father, how much importance do you put on having a living guru? In India it's part of the tradition, whereas in the West, it is not.

We have in the West the tradition of the spiritual Father, and in the early days of the monks of the desert, the *abba*, the spiritual Father. He was like the guru; it was the norm to go to him. It has remained a tradition in the Church, but not to the same extent as it is here. We rely more on the tradition of the Church, the sacraments, the Biblical teaching, and so on. We may have one who interprets it for us, but not necessarily. For Hindus, it seems you need a particular guru to teach you, to help you gain enlightenment.

What do you consider enlightenment?

I explain it like this. There are three levels of reality: the physical world in which we are involved, the psychological world—the world of the soul, mind, thought, will, desire; but reality is constituted by this body-soul, the mind and matter. And in the Oriental and ancient Christian tradition, there is a sphere beyond body and mind. That is called *atman* in Sanskrit and *pneuma* in St. Paul—the spirit. So for me, enlightenment is to go beyond the body, the sense, the mind, and to awaken to the inner spirit—the *atman* within. That is the goal of humanity.

*Have you been influenced by any of the great Indian sadhus or
mahatmas?*

I have seen some of the living teachers, but those who influenced
me most deeply all died before I came here. One was Sri Aurobindo.
For many years I studied his writings—they have a profound influence. I found him nearer to the Christian idea than any other Hindu
writer, and so his doctrine became almost part of my own thinking.
I was also greatly influenced by Ramana Maharshi. I regard him as
the most authentic Hindu saint, a man of utter purity who had realized
Brahman. I visited his ashram and the Aurobindo Ashram; both have
had a considerable influence on me. There's another, Swami Ramdas
of Anandashram near Mangalore, and there also I have stayed. He
was a pure *bhakta*, wonderfully simple. I found the atmosphere in
his ashram more devotional, certainly, than at any other ashram I
know.

Those three ashrams, which are all in measurable distance from
here, have a considerable place in my heart. Many people come to
our ashram from them, and we go to them: there's a kind of circulation.

*Father, I wonder if you have delegated your work so that the ashram
can go on should anything happen to you?*

Yes, yes! Things have developed in the twelve years we've been
here. There are three members of the community fully trained;
they could take over from me, you know. Maybe I ought to live a
little longer. . . .

*Well, of course, we hope you do. I was thinking of all the problems
that come up when an ashram is left without a spiritual dynamo.*

I am rather aware of that, so I have tried to bring the others up
so that they can take over and I should not be the one person. I am
not very attached to the idea of the guru. I don't like it all centering
on one person. The work should be diffused.

Could you say what you consider man's worst enemy?

The ego. It's the false self, you see, and it creates the persona, this
mask. It grows up partly from heredity in childhood, and gets rooted
in us. How to get beyond the ego?—we are all governed by the ego.
This causes conflict in the world, the conflict of ego. To get beyond
it is, to me, dying with Christ: you die to your ego and awake to the

resurrection, the new life. The Hindu, the Buddhist, all ancient traditions are also concerned with freeing oneself from the ego.

Father, when I started these interviews, I met an Italian woman who told me there was no purpose to life.

It depends on what she meant. She might have been a Zen Buddhist. They don't like the idea of a purpose: it's simply *to be.* I would speak in terms more of enlightenment and inner transformation, or to be one with God. That would be my goal.

Do you keep up with what is going on in the world, or do you not think it important?

One of the first things I did when I came here was to take out a subscription to *Time* magazine. I always read that. You shouldn't get isolated. I don't spend too much time on it, but to get every week the main news of what is happening in the world of politics and the world of science and art.

Could you describe the ashram's day-to-day schedule?

We rise at 5:00; we have two hours of meditation daily—5:30 to 6:30 and 6:00 to 7:00 in the evening. They are the poles of the day. We meditate on our own. Some go by the river, some in the church, some in their own rooms—just as we like. We meet three times for prayer together, and you'll see the prayer is diversified: Sanskrit chanting, scriptures, psalms. We have *bhajan* singing in the different Indian languages. We always end with *arati,* the waving of lights before the sacrament, a typical Hindu form of worship.

In the morning, we give time to work and study. Basically, it's the Benedictine tradition: prayer, study, work. An important aspect is receiving guests, also part of the Benedictine tradition. An ashram is an open community; we try to keep an atmosphere to which visitors can come, whether for an hour, a day, a week, a year.

What sort of food is served in the langar?

It's strictly vegetarian, not even eggs. We find this important. I mentioned this in the talk just now: *sattvic* food is necessary for the life of prayer. *Tamasic* food makes you heavy and dull; *rajasik* food makes too much energy and can cause violence. The *sattvic* diet of fruit, vegetables, and milk products is considered pure. For Hindus, no *sannyasi* would be considered to be living the right life if he ate meat. There's also no smoking or alcohol here; it's part of the Indian tradition, you see.

As you know, there has been a turning-away in the West from materialistic values. Could you give some advice to those wishing to break free from that life?

It's not easy. People come here searching, but have to go back. I always tell them to establish the habit of meditation—it may be half an hour a day—but apart from the daily routine, some time should be given to recollection. That establishes a center for your life. Once you have that, you can manage the world; otherwise, you get carried away by it.

You have established yourself in an idyllic setting, with peahens strolling about the jungly gardens, but—could you say something about the inner benefits you have found in this new life?

I think it is the integration of one's personality and one's whole life, and a right relation with nature—the world around. As you say, we are very blessed, we have this idyllic setting, the river Cavery, a climate where the sun shines almost all the year. Yes, it's marvelous that way. But there is also an integration in one's personal relationships—we have people coming from all over the world who we meet and share with and become enriched. And finally, and fundamentally, the relation to nature and people is integrated in the experience of God. And that is what I came to India for, and that is what is continually enriched. Here one can become more and more aware of what God is and how He is present everywhere, in everybody, in everything. Like that, one's whole life comes to a unity.

. . .

I am fairly exhausted after the interview, but supper is being served Indian style (we sit on the floor). This is followed by arati, chanting and prayers. Someone points out an Englishwoman who has left everything to spend the rest of her life at this ashram: she is over seventy, so the pull of the mystic East is not only for the young.

I am off early again in the morning for Ramanashram. A Spanish lady gives me a message for Juan, who is in room fifteen there; the message—a bit vague: "Padre esta aqui."

Traveling in India is full of surprises. Nowhere else can you be paying for your bus ticket while being asked "Does your guru give the Inner Light?" Once anyone suspects you are on your way to an ashram, deep metaphysical discussion is sure to follow. I have given up trains in favor of buses for the time being, not because buses are more comfortable (though they may be a bit quicker), but because here in the south, the buses are more frequent and reliable.

Tiruvannamalai is finally in sight—or rather, the sacred hill of Arunachala can be seen; at its foot, crowded amongst many ashrams, rests the one named after the sage who spent practically all his life there: Ramana Maharshi. He had become a legend in his own lifetime, so powerful was his magnetic presence. Paul Brunton wrote about him in the '30s, and although it is over thirty years since he left this world, that great charismatic, mystic force constantly draws people from all over the world to his ashram. Many of them were not even born thirty years ago.

And thirty years ago this ashram was like Ramana Maharshi himself, simple and compact. Now it is shining with concrete and marble; no matter, the spirit pervading the entire place is extraordinary, vivid, magical.

Not only am I given a private apartment in the ashram compound across the road from the ashram itself, I am also given the attention of Mr. N., who will look after me and see that I interview the "right" people. This makes me think there must be some "wrong" people interviewable. But not to worry, I remind myself; whoever is supposed to be interviewed will be, with or without the blessings of the helpful management.

I find Juan in room fifteen and deliver the vague message; it would be good to have a Spanish interview, but he is about to leave. So I look around the ashram, gaze up at the sacred Arunachala, and chat with a young man who explains something of the teachings of Bhagavan (this is how Ramana's followers call him). A bus full of Scandinavian tourists unloads its captives for a thirty-minute stop at the ashram. Two middle-aged ladies approach the young man and ask to photograph him. He is wearing white, rough cotton; they are in expensive machine-made copies of Indian hand-blocked prints. He tells them why he left the New York nightmare for Bhagavan; they snap away, and float back to the safety of their bus.

Part Three

In the morning, Arunachala's top is partly veiled in white mist, the only mist in a clear, brilliant sky. This is a morning mystery peculiar to the Hill; by late morning, the veil always lifts.

Arunachala is very, very old; it is mentioned in the Puranas, and the worship of Shiva is said to have begun here. Shiva's light, the story goes, was so dazzling that the devas who were worshiping him said, "Oh, Lord, we cannot look at you like this—could you not take a concrete form?" He took the form of Arunachala.

My guide, Mr. N., has his official list of interviewees ready, and he is taking me to meet one of the ashram's star attractions: Lucia Osborne, wife of Ramana's biographer and editor, the late Arthur Osborne. Mrs. Osborne, who has been here at the ashram for almost forty years, is loved and visited by many devotees.

Mr. N. explains my project. "But don't you know—I am also writing a book about ashram life," Mrs. Osborne says, laughing. "Perhaps there will be room for two," I reply. She is not sure. Mr. N. says earnestly: "But you must give an interview. His father is Polish!"

Mrs. Osborne is coy: "Are you sure his father is Polish?" Poor Mr. N. is at a loss, but I take my cue: "I, at least, am absolutely sure." "Oh, well—in that case . . . (Mrs. O. likes teasing) bring those chairs over here and let's see what comes out."

Mr. N. is in heaven.

LUCIA OSBORNE
Ramanasraman
Tiruvannamalai
29 January 1981

N ow you will have to question me: that's the only way anything will happen; I'm not good at interviews.

Very well. . . . [Mr. N. encourages me to begin.] I was just thinking that you must be Bhagavan's last living Western disciple who knew him in the flesh. How did you meet him?
The last? Oh—yes, perhaps I am. You see, my husband was teaching in the University of Bangkok; at that time, I was interested— very interested—in sculpture. I was involved in a sort of self-inquiry; it wasn't "Who am I?" but "Who are you?" Someone sent us a booklet on Bhagavan with a picture. I saw the face and thought: That's the most fascinating face I've ever seen, the most living and at the same time the most serene. It would make a marvelous subject for a sculpture. That was my first idea. I had been trying to find out who I am since childhood, wondering, asking, judging.

Where did you spend your childhood?

In *Poland*! I was born there. [Much laughter, especially from Mr. N.] In Poland, we are interested in physical beauty. I thought I was ugly when I looked in the mirror—I was horrified. There was a girl at school who was really beautiful, and I thought I would like to change with her. I didn't know about transplants then—but I was thinking, could we change the heart or brain? Then I thought: Am I the heart and brain? That started it—who am I *really*? But in Siam, I was caught up in sculpture, and all that lapsed. When we came to India, we had three small children—the youngest wasn't even a year old.

When was that?

1943—no—beginning of 1942. Our friends arranged for us to stay in Kashmir to avoid the hot season, although my husband wanted to come straight to the ashram. Since he was a schoolboy he had been interested in spirituality. It was he who brought me to it.

After a few months, the British High Commissioner said women and children shouldn't go back to Siam as the war was getting serious. My husband went back to his post, and we were offered a house here. I was then able to meet Bhagavan. I had some preconceived ideas, but when I saw him—oh! . . . *everything* fell away. His eyes were transparent, looking through you. When you sat with him, there was a feeling of oneness—everything is one, is one, is one!

Was he speaking in those days?

Yes, of course—I spoke with him; I used to show him my letters. My children were the first Western children who came here—they were made a tremendous fuss of. From that meeting, all my interest in sculpture fell away, no longer important. So that's how it started.

What sort of age were you then?

Now I'm seventy-six—I'll soon be seventy-seven—so I suppose I was, yes, thirty-eight. I have spent exactly half my life here. Now although I had no news from my husband for four years—not one letter—nothing mattered. . . .

That was because of the war?

. . . He was interned: they interned all Westerners, although he was a civilian. It may have been some sort of test for us. I sent my three-year-old son to Bhagavan—he said, "Bhagavan, please bring my daddy back safely." From that moment, I didn't worry. I am describing all this in my book, so I can't give you everything—you don't mind?

Well, he did come back safely! Can you say how he started the magazine The Mountain Path?

It was to spread Bhagavan's teaching. He felt what had already been written not suitable for Westerners. It was his service, dedicated to Bhagavan, and was an immediate success. Then one day my husband told me, "My time is up; we should prepare for it." He even told me of what he would die, and the year. He then sat down and wrote all the editorials until the issue of the magazine which would coincide with his death. He died in May 1970, but he had told me in 1968. I continued the editorial work for another four years.

How did your husband get the idea to write Bhagavan's biography? It was so inspired.

Now look—how does anyone get any ideas? Bhagavan himself inspired people to do things; this came spontaneously. That book has gone into so many editions and translations. It was *his* work.

Yes, I do understand that. What were your early days like at Bhagavan's?

We all ask ourselves why we are here, what's the purpose of life? I found from the beginning you get all the answers here—in fact, you don't have to ask any questions. By sitting in Bhagavan's presence, everything was resolved. When I came, I knew the most important thing is to find out who you really are. Those who are sincere get glimpses of that state and they know. From that, the striving to make the experience steady starts.

In Bhagavan's presence, the silence was so powerful; it was the most potent teaching. Words—he used to say—are diffused silence. So, bathed in that silence, you were, so to say, out of yourself. All your cares were thrown among the lilies, to use a beautiful expression. That was *sadhana*.

You know, after he passed away people thought we would become desolate. Nothing of the sort. To my surprise, I was walking on air; there was a feeling of elation. Do you know why? Suddenly you realized he is the inner guru dwelling in the heart, ever present. He had said, "I'm not going anywhere; where can I go?"

Since then, you can feel his presence more than ever. That's why people come here more and more. They experience that radiation. And you only have to tell him something in the heart to get help, no matter what it is.

I have been asking everyone here how they pass their day. What do you do? Can you say?

The day could have forty-eight hours . . . twenty-four are not enough. I start the day by going to the ashram between 5:00 and 6:00 for meditation—that's a beautiful time. I sit till 8:00 or 8:30. I come home, where there's plenty of visitors—as you've seen. I reply to letters. Only at night do I work on my book, till about 1:00 or 2:00 A.M.

It's very strange. I used to do the replies to the Letters to the Editor for the magazine, and I never had to rewrite anything. I would read the letter, and straightaway came the reply. It's simply as if one is nothing but an instrument of Bhagavan.

Can you share some of the more personal incidents you experienced at Bhagavan's feet?

Well—hmmm! . . . they will be doubled, because that's what I am writing about. If I hadn't started the book, I would tell you everything. Did you know Bhagavan had a tremendous sense of humor? And he was a very good cook . . . he used to cut vegetables in the kitchen. Once, the poet Muruganar—he's very well-known—was helping him, but he wasn't clever with a knife. Bhagavan said, "You are only fit to write poems." And then on another occasion, he told a lawyer, "You are only fit to argue in court."

He was so exact, and nothing was wasted. Once I saw him bend down to pick up three grains of rice from the floor. It was like seeing the Divine before you. Every act, every movement expressed this. He had a thousand faces. He had stilled the mind, but that didn't mean he was like a block of wood. On the contrary, he was not hemmed by individual thoughts. He was omniscient. He was the master of thought, not its slave.

You are telling me much more than I dared hope. Did Bhagavan perform miracles to help his followers?

Oh, yes! But they were done in an unobtrusive way—you hardly recognized them as miracles. A child was dying; the doctors had given up hope. The parents sent Bhagavan a telegram. From the moment it arrived here, that child started getting better. The parents came to thank Bhagavan. He said, "What happened?" They insisted he had saved the child. He then explained, "If the attention of a *jnani* is turned in a certain direction, Divine activity starts." That I heard him say in English. Help and grace came spontaneously. He didn't have to show anything.

A man's wife died—you know in India, we have to cremate within twenty-four hours. It was raining cats and dogs. The poor man came to Bhagavan saying, "What should I do?" Bhagavan looked through the window and replied, "It looks as if it might stop!" That was all. It stopped. That was the way he did it. Wild animals would come right up to him; there was no fear, because they knew there was nothing but peace in him.

That's such a vivid picture of him.

I usually make an awful faux pas whenever I'm interviewed. A pundit came from Pondicherry to interview me for the All India Radio. He was talking about their form of yoga, which is supposed to bring down the Divine Light from above. I said, "Hasn't it come down already?"

You were fortunate to be drawn to a living saint.

Yes, we must find a genuine guru—*genuine*. He who has not found the way himself, how can he lead, except through all sorts of byways? There are many so-called gurus, and I know a lot about them . . . but I prefer not to say any more. Those really sincere find the way. The real guru is the inner guru of the heart. The outer guru is his decoy, who creates conditions to turn you to the inner guru.

What were Bhagavan's teachings about leaving the physical body at the time of its death?

The body is but a garment—we don't die; we never die. Schopenhauer said, "There isn't an inch of ground that hasn't been a human being." Why? We drop the physical body, it turns into earth, a tree grows, that eventually turns into coal or ash; it's a perpetual *mobile*.

Our life here is like a moment in which we prepare our future state. It's very important what we do now. I had to give a speech in Bombay. I told them, "Do you know what your real bank account is? Not what you have, but what you do—that goes with you; everything else is left behind." It's important how one lives, because our last thoughts go with us at the time of this physical death; they determine our future, most definitely. This is also according to the *Tibetan Book of the Dead*. Death can be a wonderful experience; it's a transition. You can almost say that our life is death, and our death a rebirth. To go into the Beyond is our true birth.

What is encouraging is earnest effort—it never fails. People sometimes say no effort is necessary: you are there already. But we are as we are, with all our inherited tendencies. We should be as we should be. Yes, we are It already, but we have to work hard to know it, experience it. Knowing it intellectually isn't enough. If you want to learn to play the piano, or to ski, it requires effort until it becomes effortless. So why shouldn't this apply when the objective is infinity? Do you agree?

Yes, I do. I wonder—have you met during your long years in India any other enlightened saints?
No one came up to Bhagavan. He was extraordinary. Just to see him walk, just to watch his actions; they conveyed something. And I want you to really understand about his silence: it was most potent. With others, such silence could be embarrassing; . . . I won't say any more.

Did you and your husband build this house, or is it ashram property?
I built it—with four workmen, without a plan, without an architect. I built it like a sculpture: first two rooms, then the verandas, steps, arches—and the upstairs is rather nice. We just created it as we went along. The people here have such love, such devotion to God. One of the workmen was deepening the well, and I saw him folding his hands to do *namaskar*. He had found a small picture of Bhagavan in the well, floating—it must have fallen in.

Is that why you are happy to stay on in India?
Arunachala has kept me. During the war, the British High Commissioner sent us letters: The last ship is leaving for England; please make sure you are on it! My husband had been released by the Japanese, so they were doing everything to help readjust ex-prisoners. We didn't even show those letters to Bhagavan; we couldn't imagine living anywhere else. It was hard for my husband, with his high qualifications and little possibilities here. It worked out right.

But don't you think I've told you enough for today? If you like,

come to tea tomorrow—I may tell you a little more. Do come, . . .
but perhaps you will leave your tape recorder in your room. Yes?

. . .

*Mr. N. has been so much in heaven during this interview that—
in between bursts of unquiet weeping at the nostalgia evoked by Mrs.
Osborne for their great guru—he himself has asked Mrs. O. a few
questions. They were good questions, so I've let them stay in—
perhaps a third book is on the way!*

*But although Mr. N. is wonderfully pleased with this meeting, he
is unhappy indeed when he learns that I've met someone outside the
ashram—someone not on the list—who has agreed to give me the
next interview. "But how could you arrange it," he protests, "I've
been with you all the time!"*

*I explain that the same power which is looking after his ashram
affairs is looking after mine also. But he is still unhappy, so we strike
a deal: he is to be present at the interview. Mr. N. is ecstatic, I am
ecstatic, and off we go. We arrive at a large, well-built modern house,
with a large well-kept garden and a spectacular view of Arunachala.*

*As soon as I get a glimpse of the house's owner—a powerful-looking
Dutchman dressed as a sadhu—I know he will not be deterred a bit
by Mr. N.'s presence. We are taken into the Dhakshina Murthi shrine
room, placed in comfortable chairs, given cool drinks—and before
Mr. N. can ask any questions, the Dutchman nods slightly, I press
the recording button, and we are off.*

HAMSA JOHANNUS DE READE
Tiruvannamalai
30 January 1981

To start, I will say I was born in Java, which was then a Dutch colony. My childhood was spent there, but I went back to Holland for schooling. But my earliest memories are of being white amongst a mixed Melanesian-Indonesian population who had been mostly forcibly converted to the Muslim religion, while keeping many of their Hindu customs and traditions. We, as whites, were supposed to be superior and looked down on the indigenous population as a little more than monkeys but less than us. It came as an interesting shock later to recognize Hinduism as the older culture. Of my fifty-three years, I have spent few in Holland, although I have lived in Italy and Switzerland.

Where did you spend the war years?

Mostly in Japanese concentration camps. It was a shock to get back to the world of so-called peace; I thought it worse than the camps.

This was not the world I wanted. I was eighteen when I was released; there were severe adaptation problems. It was symptomatic that I decided to study psychiatry at the University of Leyden, but I soon found that wasn't the branch of science I wanted to dive into deeper. I switched to psychoanalysis and became a student of Freud.

To get a degree, I shifted to the University of Amsterdam, but there I changed again; this time, it was parapsychology. At this time, I met Hermann Hesse, to whom I dedicated my early poetry. He invited me to visit him in Switzerland, which at that time—1949–50—was a rare opportunity, as he was living in retreat. Through him, I received the desire to visit India. At the same time, I met a Dutch research scholar in comparative religion, Dr. G. H. Mees, who had started out as a student of law at Cambridge.

He was to become your teacher in India?

Yes. He had found the root of law was in religion, so he studied Buddhism, the Sufis, and Ramakrishna Paramahansa. He took a degree in comparative religion at Cambridge, and a doctorate at Leyden, with a thesis called *Dharma and Society,* in which he went into the old caste system—which wasn't hereditary. I met him in 1951, and it was he who invited me to come with him to India.

In 1936 he had toured India, as a young man of thirty-three, but in the style of the British Raj, with a huge seven-seater car, a cook, a secretary, a boy to open doors, and a man to cut wood and carry water at stopovers. While traveling in this style at Bangalore, someone told him, "There is a wonderful, crazy old man living at Tiruvanna-malai who you must meet." He went. It was Ramana Maharshi.

Within twenty-four hours he knew his search was over: he had found his *satguru!* He gave up his career, his ambitions, and settled here at Tiruvannamalai. The climate didn't, however, suit him for an all-year-round stay. He found a property by the sea in Kerala, from where he came to see Ramana regularly.

He did further writing, and produced his great work *The Revelation in the Wilderness,* consisting of three volumes on comparative symbolism, born out of a panoramic flash of the symbolism of the world. He became acquainted with much of the material through a colleague, Dr. C. G. Jung, whom he in his turn had encouraged to visit India in 1938. Jung got as far as Madras, but never visited Ramana because he had already seen the deep brown eyes of a small saint, and according to Jung, it wasn't necessary to see more. All this is documented in Heinrich Zimmer's *The Way to the Self*, with a foreword by Jung himself.

Ramana must have left the body just before you arrived.

Correct. Hermann Hesse was pushing me to go, but only when I was asked to accompany Dr. Mees and help edit his great work did I go. I had gone through a dying experience in a river near Amsterdam. Although I was a good swimmer, something went wrong; after that, I knew what I had been doing up till then was a great nonsense. I broke off all contacts, burnt all bridges, accepted Dr. Mees's invitation, and left Europe for good.

In India, Mees was better known as Sadhu Ekarasa. He took me to Tiruvannamalai, but purposely didn't say anything about the Hill or his great teacher. He knew I was a keen psychologist of twenty-four, not interested in religion. I saw all sorts of strange things going on in a place called Ramanasramam: people prostrating to a heap of earth and stones—the grave of an old man. I could have been interested in anything else but that. The conversation was beyond my field of interest. I asked Mees, "How long are we to stay in this hole?" He just said, "Let's see—maybe a day or ten!" I replied, "Good grief! **TEN DAYS HERE?**"

Later, I looked up at a brownish-grayish heap of boulders with sparse bushes, a sort of thing in between a hill and mountain, of which I didn't know the name, and more or less shook my fist, saying, "For God's sake, what am I doing here?" I began wondering—was this why I had given up my career? And I was far from satisfied by what I had seen of India so far.

Then a strange thing happened, and since I'm not psychic and not interested in these things, it struck me as doubly funny: this hill-mountain hit me in the chest—plonk—like a rock. I was breathless, speechless, thoughtless.

I went to the ashram and told anyone willing to listen to stop prostrating to the grave, for I had discovered something really wonderful, and it was That Hill! People laughed mildly, and someone said, "But this guru buried here came here *because* of That Hill!" I did some rethinking about the buried man: If that hill had spoken to him and had already spoken to me, he couldn't be a complete fool. Let's see what more we have in common.

I became interested in his teaching; within twenty-four hours, things clicked, and I knew here I would find the answers—perhaps the one answer—to the one and only question worth thinking about. In a nutshell, that still is the position today.

You have since dedicated your whole life to Ramana's way?

I have. I am satisfied that in Ramana's *sadhana* there's no such thing as progress. It's impossible to say: Today I was closer to the Truth. I am also satisfied that the *sadhana* as given by Ramana isn't a question of time, no such thing as coming closer to realization— and to think you or so-and-so are nearly realized amounts to saying you have nearly jumped over a ditch full of mud, which means you are in the middle of the dirt now.

I am satisfied that the *sadhana* is to be compared to Russian roulette: every time you sit down to dive could be the last time, and you could finish your individual existence. The number of years spent at it is irrelevant because Ramana teaches that the ego, having fantasized the concept of space by the I-thought attaching itself to your body and simultaneously creating the fantasy of time, when realization is achieved, it must be inevitably found that the *sadhana* didn't take place in time.

Muruganar, the poet and Ramana's first disciple, confirmed this indirectly when—after eighteen years of praying, dabbling, toying with "Who am I?"—I asked him, "After all these years of searching for the answer, there seems to be no progress." He smiled and said, "That *is sadhana!*"

But your response to Ramana's teachings must have changed your whole life.

I never stopped to think; perhaps it stopped me going all out for the usual things . . . career, comforts. Indirectly it changed my life by my interests becoming more centered on how I can most conveniently and most quickly die. I don't mean just the death of the body, but the death of all that makes you cling to wonderful experiences, beautiful thoughts, spiritual aspirations, and even the desire to see Light. As the desire to fall asleep has to be given up in order to fall asleep, likewise it's in surrender—in my case to Ramana—that desire for liberation will also be given up. Whether or not that is any use, the inner guru knows. And to that inner guru who has brought me to Arunachala, to Ramana, and the one or two persons I regard as the *shaktis* of Ramana, I can't be as stupid as I sometimes think I am. I must trust that instinct that holds me here in Tiruvannamalai.

In mentioning the shaktis *of Ramana, may I ask who you had in mind?*

As we choose to project our *satguru* into a certain form, that form is already the *shakti*. I think it can be compared to looking at Arunachala and Ramana's form as the *shakti* of the *satguru*, who is formless. In the case of Anandamayi Ma—who was the physical person I was thinking of just now—I can illustrate this: I met her in 1952 as I took some swamis in my car to her house. They said, "You must come in and have *darshan!*" I didn't know what that meant, but went in and had the most strange and wonderful experience of seeing eyes which were completely empty. Imagine the stupefaction of someone who throws a rock in a lake and there are no ripples. This is what happens near Anandamayi. She may react, but there's no ripple.

When I told Dr. Mees about this, he went also and he too was impressed. After three days, we took leave and returned to Tiruvannamalai, but to our amazement, there she was in Tiruvannamalai.

She had come to visit Bhagavan's ashram?

Quite so. I had the feeling there were two camps: we, the grieving disciples of the guru who had just left the body; and they, who were in proud possession of their physical guru—Anandamayi Ma. This hidden feeling of rivalry was wiped away when she sat by the *samadhi* and said, "Here is a daughter come to pay homage to her father." Then she sang *Prem Bhagavan, Prem Bhagavan,* knowing or perhaps not knowing, that Ramana was always affectionately called Bhagavan by his devotees. Anyway, both camps melted in tears and that was the end of any rivalry.

After another three days, Mees and I again took leave to go to Trivandrum by car, and a day later, she was *there.* Then after another three days with her, we took leave for the third time in ten days to go to our place by the sea. The next day we received a telegram saying she was coming to visit us. She stayed some time, and from then, whenever I was short of Ramana's direct assistance and I called for help, it was invariably provided by Anandamayi. In at least a dozen instances, I have met her by just arriving casually at a place she would be arriving the same day. That helped me to see her as the *shakti* of Ramana.

*You have been so closely associated with these great teachers, I won-
der if you yourself are now teaching?*

I have only one ambition, and that is to do nothing whatsoever.
After my thirty years here trying strenuously to achieve my aim, I
find it impossible, so one does the next best thing: while striving to
do nothing, one observes what is being asked of one while trying to
comply. This, of course, will never take the form of teaching, because
no devotee of Ramana's can do anything but repeat parrot-wise what
he has with some humility understood of the teaching of his *satguru*.
So what remains is listening, watching, which means that as long as
the identification with the body is there, rent for the body has to be
paid as work, as some kind of service with the minimum attachment
to its outcome. This means as a designer-builder, one builds, one lays
out gardens and parks, one plants forests, all of which is the outcome
of trying to do nothing.

Since Ramana has said it's not necessary to improve the world—
it's perfect as it is even though you don't see it as such—then where
is the ambition to do anything of importance?

So now you will ask me what does my day consist of? Well—I will
say—some work, some gardening, keeping in mind the Chinese prov-
erb that he who wishes to be happy for three days kills his pig and
eats it; he who wishes to be happy for three months marries; he who
wishes to be happy for all his life becomes a gardener. So I suppose
gardening is an activity that doesn't completely exclude the introspective business of watching who is doing. Then there's some writing;
some prose or poetry now and then bubbles out, so one watches that.
One speaks, one sees, one hears, while exercising a mild attempt to
keep the four types of silence: that of speech, seeing, hearing, and
the essential one, thinking.

Ramana's teaching inevitably brings one to the exercise of how to
act without thinking about it. Under those circumstances little activity
is possible. One then comes to understand by way of humility that
it's impossible to follow the guru's advice. That humility fortunately
lies close to the center of all desire, which is the desire to surrender.
The way to know is at the same time the way to surrender; the way
to surrender is at the same time the way to love, because that love
is the Self's love for Itself. Well—this takes place during most days.
Dr. Mees, my beloved and respected teacher, put all that down in
a poem called "The Tear-drops in my eyes, I offer."

Having thrown away a career to live the life of a sadhu, *is there any advice you can pass on to others?*

Even a down-to-earth Pope like John XXIII said in a private audience one Christmas or other, "This is the time of year when it's fashionable to talk about peace, but when will we all realize that as long as there are two men on this earth and only one is not at peace with himself, so long will he try to provoke a fight with the other?" He was saying peace cannot be organized, but is an individual attainment. One person wakes up; the world wakes up with him. The rest is beautification of the dream. One wakes up only from a nightmare.

It is only out of deep grief that the desire for unconditional happiness is born. And those who desire that unconditional happiness can learn from the United States and Sweden, which both have the largest national per capita income, and which at the same time show the largest percentage of suicides, drug and alcohol addicts, and people admittable to mental institutions. This shows that he who has bet on material well-being and has won it finds he has nothing!

Now you will ask how to escape? Those wanting unconditional happiness—well, tradition, including religion, used to serve a purpose . . . and it still does. But in those countries where tradition and religion have been reduced to superstition and have been thrown out, their children stand barehanded under a naked sky and have to start afresh as in the stone age. I agree with my teacher, Dr. Mees, when he said superstition is better than nothing; superstition can induce a man to inquire: What could it have meant?

In this sense, St. Paul said, "We should serve not in the oldness of the letter, but in the newness of the spirit." It's the newness of the spirit which can be rediscovered when we find the *inner* meaning of tradition and religion psychologically incorporated in the collective subconscious and popping out in our own personality; here we can find guidance, because the sages who have rigged up ritual, mythology, mystic literature, tradition and religion knew how to reach us according to our individual temperament and have taken us in the direction of where we really wanted to go in the first place.

So instead of throwing everything overboard, I would advise a reevaluation of the world's traditions and religions. If a person feels the need to go beyond the one into which he was born, there's no necessity to be converted. Ramana said clearly when people expressed the wish to become Hindus, "When a Christian says 'Yesterday I was a Christian, but now I want to be a Hindu,' it only means he has understood neither religion."

But is there any progress at all without a spiritually realized guide?
There's no forcing one's way into paradise. We have to relax. Ramana summed up his own teaching—the essence of the way to the Self—as the capacity to fall asleep, which ability everyone has. He said, "To realize the Self, you have to do practically the same as you do when you fall asleep, which everybody is not only eager to do, but knows how to do." That is—lovingly to take leave of the body, of one's feelings, of the thinking process, of all hopes of tomorrow and memories of yesterday; and lastly and most important, to take leave of the *desire* to fall asleep, *in order* to fall asleep.

This is the highway to relaxation; in other words, not to take despair, if ever it should come, seriously. Ramana has also said, "Despair and the ego itself is *in* the Self—there can never be anything *out* of it!" It's our choice whether to choose the despair that goes with seeing the ego, or to shift the attention to the Self which we love, and experience the ego as a funny accessory . . . a clown.

.   .   .

I leave Hamsa feeling very moved. Mr. N. is more confused. He is silent until he remembers to tell me that tea with Mrs. Osborne is off.

As we reach the ashram, someone hands me a note: "Don't leave Tiruvannamalai without seeing Sadhu Om." It is signed "H." Perhaps a little more intrigue is called for!

At 4:00, "H" (who is Hamsa, of course) sends a messenger, who takes me to a nearby farmhouse; there, on an upper floor, a young Englishman talks to me about his guru, a direct disciple of Ramana. The guru comes out—humble, aware, sparkling: it is Sadhu Om. I am filled with happiness, as one automatically is in the presence of a high being. The messenger asks the Sadhu question after question; the Sadhu, all attentiveness, listens, reflects, smiles. Advice pours out; it is the advice of his own great guru, but it comes out fresh, with tremendous living force. That's the advantage of the living guru: he can contact us however low we are, however dull, however hopeless.

I return to the ashram and try to creep into my room unnoticed, but it is too late; Mr. N. has discovered my absence. He sees the book under my arm (I was able to buy Part II of Sadhu Om's The Path of Sri Ramana), and the kitty-cat is out of the bag. He is reproachful; but what can one do? "Come," I say, putting my arm through his, "Mrs. Osborne can't give us tea, but I can!" Smiles, peace.

But Kirsti—yet another unofficial interviewee—arrives. I have been told that she will have a wonderful story, and perhaps she does, but she is so Finnish that I can't understand any of her lovely whispers. She is sweet and gentle, though, and does her best, and by now Mr. N. is past caring, so we are all ecstatic again. I love this place.

In the morning I hand over my donation in the ashram office, and receive old copies of The Mountain Path. *And as I leave, here comes Lynn, an Australian interior decorator who has been taking a round-about tour of ashrams on the way to see her guru, Sai Baba. I too am on my way to Sai Baba's ashram, but by the direct route, so hopefully we shall meet again.*

But it is uncertain if I shall even get there. . . . the bus has broken down. I am standing by the road in the middle of nowhere: is this a desert? Nightfall. But having squeezed myself into a local bus, we are finally limping into Bangalore. Here I am to stay with old friends: Raj is a brigadier, so their house in the cantonment is imposing with military status; Sarla is the daughter of Bhadra Sena, whom I have known and revered from the moment I first set foot in India.

But the imposing house is already draped in darkness—I am four hours late. Then I see a car plowing down the drive; Raj and Sarla are going to a party. They pull me into the car, reverse, switch on twenty lights, show me my room, order hot water, and again into the Bangalore darkness they disappear.

I sleep wonderfully well, and by the morning, Raj has all the Sai Baba information ready. A direct bus will take me from Bangalore to Puttaparthi, birthplace of Sai Baba and site of his main ashram.

I arrive after five bumpy hours to find a stage-set dream city, sprung up in quasi-desert country; everything is sparkling pink, blue, and pale yellow, and at sunset, the stillness and vivid color are Dali-esque. The bus unloads its crowd of passengers, all devotees of Sai Baba, all joyous in anticipation of Baba's darshan. They are of all shapes and ages, and they rush through the compound—which contains colleges, hospitals, huge blocks of devotee accommodations, temples, student hostels, a bank, Baba's house, Baba's gardens, and an enormous open space where Baba gives his walking darshans. Everyone has rushed from the bus to the ashram accommodation office, where two unrushable clerks are doling out rooms.

I explain my mission. Yes fill out the forms read the instructions don't leave the ashram until your visit is up and you have to share a room. Right, but don't you have a single room? Yes that will be extra. Right. Please get your meal tickets at the other office don't eat outside the ashram please pay in advance. Right, but can you tell me who to approach about the interviews? The American in room C-629 will know.

And he does, too. He has been in the ashram some years, knows who is talkable to and who isn't, and has an alarming number of mattresses in his room. Picking one up, he takes me to my room, which is large and newly built and has nothing in it but four walls, a floor, and a ceiling. This really is simple living.

He throws down the mattress—all for me?—and gets down to business: No interviews can be taken without permission from Dr. Bhagavantum, Baba's secretary, and he left the ashram this morning for a day or two, or maybe three.

If such an important person is away, there must be a deputy secretary one can approach? Of course not! Deadlock.

Then, a brainwave from my new friend. (I can't give his name because he later gave an interview, thus breaking the rules himself, so I have called him Sir, which pleased him.) The brainwave: to ask Baba himself for permission when he comes out for his darshan. Great! Sir helps me write a note, which I am to pass to Baba should Baba wish to accept it. Well—what can I do but hold it out and try? It requests his blessing for the book and permission to interview a few of his Western disciples.

Baba is beginning his slow progress along the segregated lines of breathless, expectant disciples. (Males and females are much separated here; they don't even eat together in the hangar-like canteen.) Baba is in full-length vibrant pink—perhaps to match the decor— and is smiling and gracious, and is actually taking my note! Sir gasps with delight. Baba stops. He addresses me, "I'll see you later." He is all sweetness, and in response to a devotee's plea for something or other, makes a circular movement with his outstretched hand, which

*is turned downward. From his fingers and right in front of my eyes,
he lets fine powdered ash fall into the open palms of the blissed-out
devotee. Baba smiles at me again, and moves on.*

*"Did you see that?" Sir later yells, almost blissed-out himself. "He
did that specially for you." And indeed, Baba hadn't repeated this
mini-miracle again throughout the rest of his fifteen-minute peram-
bulation, despite the fact that thousands of open palms were silently,
imploringly held up to him as he passed.*

*But I am trying to be practical, so I ask Sir what will happen next.
Sir is confident. "You'll see—he knows everything. . . . He didn't
have to read the note:* **HE KNEW.** *" Quite, but—still trying to be
practical—when can we start the interviews? And what did he mean
when he said he would see me later? After trying out many inter-
pretations, we decide it is safest to wait and see.*

*But . . . how late is later? After four hours of waiting, I am not
altogether convinced that Sir is correctly interpreting the Divine Will.
Sir proposes a new plan: I am to hand Baba another note during his
morning darshan. Well, why not? But the next morning, Baba walks
unsmiling right past me; he ignores the note. Sir remains optimistic;
all I have to do is wait until the afternoon darshan and hand Baba—*

Another note?

*Well, at last Sir is getting the message. He is thinking deep, real
deep. Dr. Bhagavantum never returned, may never return, and here
we are, holding out notes and getting nowhere. But Sir is not the
sort of person who will let a friend down: we will start the interviews,
he proposes, and then get permission. A daring thought! I urge Sir
to hurry and find some interviewees, before he changes his mind.*

*Soon enough he produces two Germans, and our bold plan is
underway.*

JOACHIM PETERS AND ULI STECKENREUTER
Prasanthi Nilayam
Puttaparthi
5 February 1981

*A*s *you both wish to give the interview together, let's start with Joachim, as you are older—right?*

JOACHIM: Uli is like my son. We are both from Germany. I am fifty-two years old, but when I was twenty-four, I had a strange spiritual experience—it suddenly happened although I didn't know about these things. I fell down unconscious one afternoon and was in an ocean of light. In this light, slowly, a figure appeared, and I knew it was a divine being; first I saw it from the backside, turning; the face was brown and the eyes made me afraid. I thought it was Jesus, but couldn't understand why he had a dark complexion. From then I knew there were other levels of consciousness, and I started reading much about spiritual things. That went on for some years together with my professional life.

Can you say what it was?

I was an actor. In 1972, I decided to stop the reading and go to India for a guru, a divine incarnation. I came to Sai Baba almost immediately, and I had the feeling: I have found my guru. So quick! After a few nights, I had a dream—I didn't know then that when one dreams about Baba, Baba really appears; he says nobody can dream about him if he doesn't want it.

In this dream, I sat on a prayer mat, Baba stood beside me and gave me something to drink—it was tasteless—then we both went up to the sky like two flames merging in a cloud of bliss and love and incredible joy. In the morning I was told that the day before was a special day, and in former years, Baba had distributed *amrita*, but this year he didn't. I didn't grasp the dream properly, nor the meaning of the drink, although I was told it was the nectar of immortality.

A week later, I had my first interview with Sai Baba—it was with a group. He materialized things and was all love; he asked if I had any questions, so I said, "Yes, one." He said, "You want to talk? Come." And he took me behind a curtain, and there he turned completely into the Divine Mother, full of sweetness. I didn't have to narrate my dream; he knew—he said, "No birth again!" I couldn't grasp it still. He repeated, "No birth again—*moksha*, liberation." I was so happy I started weeping. I felt Baba had taken loads of karma off my shoulders. I was a changed being.

Did you have to go back to Germany?

I went after a few weeks. But Baba was with me. I wasn't able to get work, but was in a blissful state. Then every year for eight years, he brought me back, coming, coming, changing, changing my character. Sometimes he gave me some treatments—he never looked at me for half a year, but the very moment I was back in Germany, I was brimful of bliss, so that I would know the Baba in the body was part of the Baba in the heart; and he filled me completely.

Now this last year Baba has told me not to go back, to stay permanently. I hope I will become less and less and merge in him like those two flames in the dream.

When you said your character changed, what did you mean?

I was a chain smoker, drinking alcohol, with many love stories; and I was eating meat.

Can you now give an account of Sai Baba's teachings?

He says in the end there is nothing but God. He puts stress on thinking good, seeing good, speaking good, doing good. He says we should do *sadhana* and *sadhana* and *sadhana*, but I have the feeling it is Baba who does the *sadhana* for us—he is working from day to night on us. He changes and shapes us inside by dreams and so on.

He pays your karmic debts?

He destroys them. Once, we were all singing *bhajans* on the Maha Shivratri; at sunrise, he came into the hall, delivered his discourse. But this single sentence remains in my mind, "This night I have taken sins from you."

He washes away much dirt. Many people here get diseases and we are never bothered about it, as we see it as a form of purification. Should he wish it, he can take it all away. I used to think I knew Baba—now I know I know nothing—yes, I know he is love incarnate. He is always caring for us. When I had to look for a place to stay here last year, I was walking in a street and a man on a motorcycle asked me, "Do you want a flat?" I saw it was a new-built house, so I rented it immediately. Just like that.

How do you spend your time? Do you do any seva?

No. I used to read like a rat; this habit has stopped. Baba makes one think of him twenty-four hours a day—I am always busy with Baba, busy being quiet, listening to the heart, to the peace, to the bliss. That's the occupation one can see from the outside. Oh, I should tell you that the vision I had when I was twenty-four—when I lost consciousness—was Baba; he himself told me so.

Now should we hear what Uli has to tell us?

ULI: I am twenty-seven now. After school I didn't know what to do, so I ended up in the police force in Germany. After two years, I was sick of the discipline, and—having read Hermann Hesse—I said, "Enough! Let me go to India"—just like that. I was eighteen and didn't know about saints, but after five days in India, I ended up with a saint—the teacher of Ram Das, Neem Karoli Baba. I stayed with him for two months; I didn't do any *sadhana*, but he changed my whole life. I didn't even have any devotion for him. I just went because I had met someone who said, "Let's go there; he is nice and we can eat free." I had an incredible experience there. I never spoke to him—rather, he never spoke to me, except after six weeks. He said, "What's your name?" I said, "Uli." He said, "Cooli? Ah, work!"

That was the only conversation I had with him. But he was working on me on subtle levels. He understood what was in my mind, what I wanted—there was some communication *there*. But at that time, I didn't know who he was. Through my cultural background, I was very narrowed in. He just opened me up. I then spent time in America, sort of a free life, but I met some Sai Baba devotees whom I liked. When I came back to Germany, I met more Baba devotees, and as Neem Karoli Baba had died, I decided I should come to India again. First I saw other saints, then came to see Baba. At the first meeting, he just looked into my eyes, and I knew he was the highest being I had met. I had been with about ten saints. But he never talked to me, like Neem Karoli Baba. He made lockets for others, but ignored me. Eventually, he asked my name, and when I told him, he said, "Cooli? Ah, work!"

I stayed with him four months, and that was the only conversation I had with him. No, I remember I did have one other—the summer course was going on and everybody had to have a badge to get in. There were a few without badges—I was one—so we couldn't get in; we were sitting outside waiting for Baba to arrive and help us. He came, looked at us, told someone, "Give him a badge, him, him, him," and so on—but again he ignored *me*. He was so godlike, I was so shy, I could never approach him, but he lingered as if to let me know that if I wanted to speak, speak! All I could say was, "Summer Course!" He said, "Achha?" as if to say—oh, you can talk, but also at the same time it was like an embrace.

You mean he never gave you a badge?

No! I had to stay outside. You just can't get in without one. Anyway, I had to go back to Germany, but after three months I was back again. Again he completely ignored me. Then I started thinking: I need another guru, I need a guru who talks to me, I need a guru I can relate to—this is nothing! I even remember once he was driving by in his car; to the person left of me, to the person right of me he smiled and waved, and he didn't even *see* me. I thought, what's wrong with me, what's wrong with me? Then I was very sick—stomach trouble—and down, depressed—and about to leave and look for another saint. I was sitting at *darshan*, really down physically and mentally; Baba came out, but I thought: Well, you are God—I can't go to a doctor because you can cure me if you want to in an instant.

He looked at me—in the area of my stomach—and said, "Go in!" and gave me an interview. Then—from then on, for a year—he gave me so much attention, talked to me, made me feel I was close to him. He made me [manifested] this locket I wear—even the chain —at that first interview, and said, "You have pain—I'll take it away; you want to talk to me this evening?"

I was so happy, but all day long I was also confused by this sudden love. In the evening, he said, "How are you now?" I said, "A little confused." "*Confused?*" he said, "If you are confused, I won't talk to you." He started to walk away. I yelled out, "It's much better now," so he came back, saying, "Don't be confused; be happy." From then on he has given me many interviews and made me this special ring.

JOACHIM: You should tell how he wanted to get you married.

ULI: Baba was marrying an American couple, blessed them, made them rings and showered them with rice—brown rice—coming out of his fingers. After he had given them a talk on what marriage means, he turned to me, saying, "Now *you* are going to get married." I cried, "Baba, no, no! I don't want to get married—I really don't want to." He said, "I am going to marry you to God!"

You must have many other illustrations of Baba's sense of humor.

JOACHIM: There was a Thread Ceremony; on the platform, three or four pundits were reciting mantras, but Baba was walking up and down, spraying from his finger tips flower petals and such things. The pundits became excited and called out, "Shiva! Shiva!" And Baba turned round and asked, "Yes?"

Baba has been wearing his special curly hairstyle, and some people get a shock when they see it for the first time. Two Westerners were talking about it, saying you have to be careful with such a style not to get lice. Some days later, they had an interview with Baba, who said as he bent his head, "You have to be careful with such hair— it's so easy to get lice." And there they could see innumerable small snakes.

ULI: Oh, do you remember when two brothers were talking about Baba actually wearing a wig? That evening at *darshan*, as he passed them he tugged at his hair and then went on. And then on another occasion, he took out a white handkerchief as he passed someone, rubbed it very hard against his lips, and showed it to the person without any mark on it. That man told me later that he had actually been telling his friend that Baba uses lipstick. He does these funny things, but they always have significance.

JOACHIM: Once Baba said that Krishna wore his hair like he does, but with a cloth round it. He put a towel on his head like a turban to show us, then he waved his hand and produced a huge emerald —about the size of a small egg—saying, "This stone belonged to Krishna's grandmother." He placed it on the turban and then handed it around so that we could all see it. Then, taking it back, he said: I have to send it back; it is part of the Crown Jewels and the guard will get in trouble if someone notices that it is missing. It disappeared from his hand, just like that.

Have any of these objects been verified?

JOACHIM: There is a good example in Howard Murphet's book about Baba. A New York gentleman was over here and Baba materialized an expensive piece of jewelry which had a shop label and price tag on it. He gave it to the man, who on his return to New York immediately went to the shop on Fifth Avenue. He showed the piece of jewelry and asked if the record of sale could be shown to him. Surely enough it could be traced, and the assistant said, "I can never forget the man who bought it—he had his hair sticking out in all directions and was wearing a red robe and he paid cash." The date of sale was the same as the day Baba had given the piece to him.

I suppose Baba manifests objects to teach you something.

ULI: Ach, all the time. Baba made a ring appear. He showed it to someone and asked, "What kind of ring is this?" He said, "It is gold with an emerald." This was confirmed by other people there. Then Baba took it back, blew on it—phuur!—showed it to everyone, and they all said, "Oh, it's now silver with a diamond!" He did this several times—blowing and showing—and the ring had changed every time. Then Baba said, "See, Baba can change any material in the universe into another, but to change one of you Westerners is very hard."

. . .

*After this interview, I ask Sir if he can arrange an interview with
a woman. A woman? Certainly not—we would have to have very
special permission for that.*

*At the next darshan, Baba floats past me again; he is very loving
with some old people in wheel chairs. When it is over I catch sight
of Lynn, the Australian interior decorator; she has finally made it to
see her guru. She laughs when she sees me, but on the ashram
grounds, we cannot speak. As we pass, she whispers, "Meet me in
the X---Café in half an hour."*

Go out of the ashram precincts? To see a woman?

*We meet. We see others unlawfully talking, smoking, even tea-
drinking (I can't see any other vices . . .); they too have sneaked out.
Lynn's first question, "Aren't you by this time sick of all these holy
ashrams? I can't bear them! I love Baba, but this ashram . . . !" We
have tea, and Lynn tells me she is taking a taxi in two days back to
Bangalore. That fits my plans also, for I have a berth booked on the
night train, so I must get back to Bangalore. But dare we leave
together?*

*Returning to the ashram (Lynn and I carefully stagger our arrivals),
I make one last try. Dr. Bhagavantum still has not returned. Sir is
sure that something will happen to make me stay on until Dr. B.'s
return, but I know that no matter what happens, I will share a taxi
with Lynn the following day. So I decide it is time to be even bolder:
I walk right into Baba's private house.*

*I don't get far. An elderly pundit-doctor stops me. I explain I have
been here three days, must leave tomorrow, and want only a Yes or
No about the interviews. He says no one but Dr. Bhagavantum can
go in and ask such a question. Yes, I know that! But can no one else
help me?*

*When you pour out your heart to an Indian, he always responds.
"There is only one thing left," the learned pundit tells me. "You go
across the road to the post office and send Baba a personal telegram
stating the case; he must open that himself!" With a wave of his hand
he points the direction.*

*This at least is better than just sitting about waiting. I find the tiny
P.O. a minute's walk away, take a form from the postmaster, and ask*

is it possible to have a telegram delivered to Baba before the evening darshan. Lovely smile from the postmaster: "It will be delivered by me personally." I write, pay, leave, now totally enchanted with the situation.

At the darshan we all sit in neat, long lines. The discipline is extraordinary, as is the silence and patience of the waiting thousands. Baba is one hour late—surely he has received the telegram! I am in a euphoric state—but I can't understand if it's because of the comic-opera situation (the baritone rushing in at the last moment with a telegram proving the about-to-be-banished poet is in fact the tenor's long-lost brother!), or if it's the descent of some blissful resignation.

Baba walks past me so slowly. I have the much-crumpled note in my hand. But I can't hand it to him. I am filled with tremendous happiness—laughing inside. I only hope it doesn't show outside; in these solemn moments it is important to observe propriety. Baba walks on. All is as it should be. The opera won't have a hammy ending, for the rejected one will withdraw of his own accord, happy to find a lovely Australian soprano waiting to mount the taxi with him. Lynn and I drive off into the morning sunrise!

In the center of Bangalore, I am able to collect the three rolls of film I have left for developing. I study the proofs of the photos I have taken so far. Relief—at least the camera is working. Lynn flies off to Bombay; I place myself in the train to Kerala.

It is yet another long journey. Just before lunch the following day, I arrive at Anandashram, near the town of Kanhangad. And here is Swami Satchidanand who signs his letters "Ever your Self," greeting me. Mother Krishnabai knows about the book, but at the moment there are no devotees here. Mother has not thought it a good time for Western followers to come to the ashram.

No interviews? I've come all this way for nothing? But as I walk toward the canteen, a little distance ahead I see the back view of a familiar form. It is that tireless ashram traveler, Charan Das. Within ten minutes, he has filled me in with the latest ashram gossip and the movements of the newly married Kalidas and Uma—they are going to spend the summer in Mussoorie, near my home! He has a list of ten more ashrams for me to visit, and at least six more West-erners living all over India. One is a nun who is writing a thesis on unknown women saints; another, a maharani who has two gurus and whose grandmother was a Romanian Gypsy; yet another works as a doctor in one of the Rama-Krishna hospitals and meditates all night.

Then I ask, "Now come along. You surely are not going to let me go away from this place without taking one interview—can't you give me yours?" Perhaps. . . .

But we are rushing to see Mother Krishnabai, for she allows her few visitors into her room after lunch. She is not in good health, but I see at once a radiant, smiling, transparent figure of great stillness and peace. She gazes at me with much love and my heart is filled with pain; my mind stops planning. Back again to absorbing! . . . and such quiet, dynamic force is being released. This is the eternal beauty, the essence no book can do justice to: the physical presence of a saint, which bathes one in a fragrance not found anywhere else.

There are some questions about the book, about the journey. She speaks about her great guru, Swami Ramdas; she prostrates before his large photograph; she holds one of his books to her forehead and presents it to me. She is the perfect disciple. There is absolutely no sign of rules and restrictions in this ashram; it is small and intimate and above all, loving.

In the evening, I walk alone in the simple grounds. And later, after much herb tea, Charan Das relents and begins his interview. He has had an eventful ashram-to-ashram life, and—his memory being vivid and flawless—no detail is spared. After midnight, when we stop for more tea, I realize we have only covered the first two years of his life in India. I am beginning to think that Charan Das needs half a book all to himself.

By 2:30, when it is all over, I know that Charan Das needs a whole book to himself. Or at least, he will have to go into the next collection, for there is no way to abbreviate his marvelous story.

The next morning, I take the local train to Mangalore, and from there, the plane direct to Bombay. My itinerary had called for a more circuitous journey, but I am beginning to feel physically exhausted, and in need of less excitement. From Bombay airport, I take a taxi, and in ten minutes, we have reached the Hare Krishna Temple and I am booking a room at the super deluxe hotel which is part of the temple complex.

The service is perfect and I soon meet the project manager, who is Swiss and a disciple of Srila Prabhupad, the founder of the Hare

Krishna Movement. He is a busy, much-in-demand person, but is happy to know about the interviews I have already taken; he agrees to ask the president of the temple if he will give one. Then, as my newfound Swiss friend is telling me in passing about his own life, I stop him and ask if he won't give me an interview also. "No, no!" he answers at once—"I am not important." But he is because he is full of humility and not at all like a businessman, even though he is behind an executive desk. Finally he agrees to the interview, because he feels it important to represent all walks of life and backgrounds.

CHITRAKARA DAS ADHIKARY
Iskcon
Bombay
10 February 1981

I was born and raised in Switzerland in a small village. My father is an executive of a mill. Later on I went to college, studied the arts, but before I decided on which profession to take up, I shifted to another school—the Arts School of Zurich—and took photography and film-making for three years. After I graduated there, the school itself employed me, so I was able to work in the Art Museum of Zurich, which was attached to the school. After one year, I started traveling, and it was about nine or ten years ago I first came to India—I was twenty-one then. I was looking for some ideals in life. Even in my Zurich days, I had come into contact with Eastern philosophy, mostly Taoism, and had read several books on it. I had even taken some yoga lessons, and I had more or less given up meat-eating. When I arrived in Delhi, I decided to go from village to village on a tour, and for that purpose I purchased a bicycle.

That's a very original way to see the country. How far did you get?

I wanted to see the villages on my way to Bombay—that's about one thousand miles away—but I never made it. It took me almost a day just to get out of Old Delhi. There were no road signs. After ten days of cycling, with stops in-between, I felt this wasn't the best way to travel. I looked at my map for the next town—it was Mathura—and went there to sell the cycle. There was only one hotel—very small, very nice, on the banks of the Jamuna. I stayed there, but became attracted by the river and the *sadhus* sitting by it and the atmosphere—it was all overwhelming. I remember taking a bath in the river and just sitting there. I had an immense experience of satisfaction just by sitting in that peace.

My ideal had been the Chinese way of Buddhism, so I couldn't understand why the river affected me so much. I tried to analyze where this happiness was coming from; it wasn't from the company of beautiful girls, I hadn't smoked any marijuana, and I didn't have a good meal behind me—there were none of the usual sense-gratifications. My conclusion was that it was the river itself that was the cause of the incredible happiness, and it must be very special. I wrote a poem on the beauty of this river which was giving me so much peace and sweetness. Then, as I walked through the streets, some *sadhus* approached me and said, "You know this is the birthplace of Lord Krishna?" I asked, "Who is Lord Krishna?"—I really didn't know.

They took me to see Krishna's birthplace and told me to go to Vrindavan, as that was also associated with him. I went by bus; I still couldn't figure out who was this Krishna everyone was talking about. As soon as I got out of the bus, I had fifty beggars on me. Still, I was able to see some of the temples—of course, they don't let Westerners inside. I was fascinated, but I didn't relish all the beggars.

You didn't stay there?

No, I went south as I planned, but I was always remembering Mathura and the river. I was telling everyone, if they go north—go see Mathura. Then I arranged it on my way back to be in Mathura for the festival of Holi, which is very famous there. There was this huge procession through the bazaar, with bullock carts and white bulls covered in purple, green and red dust, and people throwing color everywhere—it was out of another world. I was pulled onto one of the carts where they were singing *bhajans* and playing instruments, and I was given some cymbals which I had to also play with them. Afterwards, when I got down from the cart, I had to dance with the people. Then I got pulled onto another cart, which had two big barrels of colored liquid and two boys were dressed up as Radha and Krishna in fantastic costumes, and they had two pumps which I had to keep filled from the barrels. As we rode through the streets, the crowds got splashed with this color. There were elephants in the procession, ridden by *sadhus*. At one point one of these *sadhus* passed me and gave me such a long look that I nearly took off—I was so excited, so out of this world.

Were any other Westerners there at the time?

No, not one. I was the only one in the town, and the people appreciated that. You probably know that during this festival, everyone embraces each other and puts color on you; well, I had about one inch of color on me by the time it was all over. My clothes were completely finished. I went to the bazaar to get new things. Here I met a small old man with glasses and a stick—it is still a mystery to me who he was. He tapped me on the shoulder—and this in itself was like an electric shock. Later I understood he must have been a *vaishnava sannyasi*.

He spoke to me in perfect English and started preaching to me. He said, "You have been drawn to the place of Lord Krishna; you should always pray to the Lord and you will reach perfection." He went on like this for five minutes and told me I should chant the holy names of God and that I could come to see him at his ashram. I very much liked him, but he turned around and walked away; I could see all the people paying obeisance to him. For two or three days, I tried to find out who he was, but I never did, and eventually I left Mathura with this wonderful impression.

You stayed on in India though?

No, I went back to Europe, and as soon as I got there, I wanted to travel again. Instead of buying a ticket for the East, I landed up in Canada, thinking: As I have seen the East, I should now see the West. I thought maybe I would work there, but although I got an immigration standard visa, I didn't like it, and moved on to the United States, which was a tremendous cultural shock—especially California. The society was so animalistic. I met all these characters; they were so burned out. I became depressed and decided I would never come back to this place.

After only ten days, I went to Vancouver Island, where I got a job in a studio and wanted to save money so that I could come back to India; I was so homesick. A little later, I met some Hare Krishna devotees in Winnipeg; they had just started a Center there. They gave me a *Back to Godhead* magazine, and as I felt homesick for India, I went with them to their temple. I had read some books of Srila Prabhupada, but no one had preached to me. In the temple I was told I should chant sixteen rounds of Hare Krishna *mahamantra*, and they explained the principles. From that moment on, I followed their program and attended all the *pujas*. I felt at peace and relieved, and after only three months, I received my first initiation.

In those days, Guru Maharaj was still alive. Can you say how you were given initiation and what it signifies?

The temple president felt I was qualified for initiation, so after consulting with the zonal secretary, they sent a letter explaining everything to Srila Prabhupada, who accepted me. He gave me my new name; a fire ceremony was performed and a *japa mala* which Srila Prabhupada had sent specially for me was presented. It is usually not given until after six months, but in my case, it was given in less than three.

I still had a great desire to come back to India, so every day I would pray in the temple, "Dear Guru Maharaj, please arrange that I can serve you in India." Ten days later—at 6:00 in the morning— a phone call came from the zonal secretary saying he had just received a letter from Srila Prabhupada, asking that two boys should be sent immediately to India. I was selected. At 11:00 the same day, I was on the plane to Toronto, then two days later I was on my way.

How old were you then? Was Guru Maharaj actually in India?

I was twenty-three—oh yes, he was here in Bombay. I was so happy, as it was my first meeting with him.

Can you describe what he was like and how he taught?

He was very grave—yes, that is the right word—but in his activities he was unmatchable. For example, at 6:00 sharp every morning we would walk with him on the beach, and even for us young boys it was hard to keep pace with him—he was so fresh and walked so fast.

He was already over eighty. The walks were wonderful because he taught us at every step; he was very frank and yet intimate.

How many of you would go with him?

Here is a picture on my desk of us all together from those days— only five or six. He would preach all the time; wherever he looked he would see Krishna, and take everything he saw in front of his eyes as a springboard to teach. Whatever he was doing during the day would be turned into a lesson. I remember once we passed a tree by the road, and at one place under a branch was an accumulation of bird droppings. He stopped and said, "Just see, even birds are attached to their home—they will only sit on a particular branch—so not only are humans attached to family and home, but birds also." And he used it to preach about the strong pull of attachment to this physical world. Whatever he saw he would put in relation to the human plight and would preach.

After the walk, we would go to the temple for *guru puja* and the *darshan* of the deities. Then he would go to his quarters, where we would serve him breakfast before he started work on his correspondence—his instructions are there in thousands of letters. He had over one hundred centers all over the world, so you can imagine how many letters that brought in. At noon, he took *prashadam*, followed by a rest for about one hour. After that, he gave *darshan* for visitors till about 7:00, when he went to the temple to deliver the lecture. In the evening he would speak to his disciples until about 10:30, when we would go to rest—but that was the time he stayed up to translate his books. At the most, he took one or two hours of rest during the night, so except for the one other hour of rest during the day, he was either preaching or translating.

During that period he was working on his seventeen-volume translation of the life and teachings of Chaitanya Mahaprabhu. So many different persons came to see him, yet each one felt Srila Prabhupada relating to him; he was so encouraging, so personal. It was all so rare and wonderful.

Were you able to take any further initiations?

After a few months, he personally gave me the second initiation. This is given when a certain amount of preaching has been done by the aspirant. At the second initiation the Brahmin thread is given to him, which signifies that he is now a preacher, and from that time onwards he is allowed to do *puja* in the temple. It is usually given about one year after the first initiation; it may take longer—it depends how one makes progress. Then a silent *mantra* is spoken into the right ear of the disciple and the guru puts the thread on the disciple's body. From then on, I was engaged in preaching in Bombay.

Did you accompany Guru Maharaj on any of his travels?

No, I stayed back in India.

Now can you tell me how this great temple was built?

We were facing difficulty obtaining permission, but it came in 1975 and the temple was built and finished within two-and-a-half years. Our Guru Maharaj was eager to complete it quickly, so work went on day and night. Three or four hundred people were chipping marble the whole time until it was finished, and even today I can hardly believe it was done so quickly.

You have the title of Project Manager. What does that mean?

After all the building stopped, the question came up as to who would manage the administration. Some of us had to sacrifice part of our preaching, and I was asked to do the administration for the guest house. By Krishna's grace, it has become very successful and we receive guests from every part of the world. Our fifty rooms are nearly always booked all year round by people like you who come here already interested in spiritual life. That is our aim: to provide facilities for serious persons who wish to have the right atmosphere, but of a high standard. The dining room has also become popular with the people of Bombay and many take the opportunity of eating Krishna *prashadam*.

We are also setting up a model Krishna-consciousness community, a whole village, because we are always preaching about the ideal way of life so we want to practice it and demonstrate that it can be done. I spend three days a week outside Bombay on this project. The village will be self-sufficient. There is so much we have to do, as hardly anyone anywhere is giving spiritual education, so we are spreading Krishna-conscious culture—the need is great and our work small, although we get up before 4:00 each morning and keep going till 9:00 or 10:00 at night.

You would never change your life now or go back to Switzerland? After all, it's the cleanest, best-organized country in the world.

If I ever think about it, just to put my feet outside India, I get cold shivers down my back. Once one has tasted a little Krishna-consciousness or any other spiritual consciousness, there is just so much more space in India—and the environment is more conducive to living a real life. In the West, it is more difficult for an individual to pursue any of his ideals. That was the main reason I joined this movement: I was an idealistic person, but I always found myself in the position of a hypocrite because I couldn't live up to the standard of my philosophy. So when I met that first Hare Krishna devotee, I sensed: This person is not a hypocrite; he is living up to his teachings.

When I joined, I had a feeling of great release. After living here for eight years, I have become so used to the culture, the environment and the people. Sometimes I have to go to the airport to meet someone and am shocked by the Westerners—they are so gross I cannot relate to them. You have met my wife—she is an Indian devotee and we have a boy one year old now. I would never even *like* him to see the Western countries as they are now. For that reason, I have actually applied for Indian nationality.

. . .

At 8:00 P.M, H.H. Giriraja Swami, President of the Hare Krishna Temple, is to have a half hour free for the interview, and I am waiting in Chitrakara's office—thinking that someone has told the president I am there. At 8:15, with half the interview time gone, I knock on the president's door. He is talking to three secretaries, answering two phone calls, and rebuking me for being late. How to explain?

No time now for the interview. Tomorrow? He may have to go to Madras. When will he know? 5 A.M. Right, I will be there to find out yes or no. Exit.

5:00 A.M. The president is not going to Madras. Come back at 11:00. 11:00—I go into his room. Horrors! "I told you to come at 11:30." I wait. Finally he says in a tired voice, "I really don't know if I can speak—I was hoping that at least I could rest on the way to Madras." He is a young American—about thirty—and obviously working under stress. I tell him this should not be any bother to him, but of course I would like him to give the interview.

Then he aims a lot of questions: Am I interested in the Hare Krishna movement? Do I have a guru? Why? Then he announces, "If I give the interview I will have to criticize the many false gurus and false teachings." I explain that is not the purpose of the book. He replies, *"I must speak the truth!"* I hold on: *"Speak the truth about your way and your guru; leave the others to drown if they are drowning."* He doesn't like that. *"I know why I can't give you the interview,"* he says suddenly. *"It's because I can't change you!"*

This knocks me out. I say that I am willing to change to anyone else's way if he can show me he has achieved enlightenment. Silence. I then make him smile a bit by pointing out that if no one will give me an interview at each ashram I visit unless he changes me to his way, I am going to end up a psychological mess.

In the end, after more negotiations and delays, the president agrees to give the interview, and is actually very mild; he criticizes no other gurus and speaks lyrically about his own, but for other reasons, the interview can't be used in this book. We part with respectful smiles.

At last it is time to head northward again, but there seems to be little—no!—chance of getting on the Rajdhani Express to Delhi. I arrive at the great Bombay station and plead my case, wait for cancellations; the afternoon train leaves, full. The night train will also be full. The official tells me to try again in three hours.

I leave my luggage in the baggage room and, carrying my small case with the recorder and camera, I set out to look for a bookshop, as I want to get Nisagardatta Maharaj's book I Am That. I've been told that Maharaj is very ill, so I had not planned to approach him, but as I have this time to spare, I take a taxi to his place. Then— what can I lose?—I climb a dilapidated stairway (this isn't one of the better parts of Bombay) and find a small gathering at the feet of a simply clad, very ill-looking man of seventy.

The room is tiny, but I manage to sit down on the floor. Nisagardatta looks hard at me but is in too much pain to speak. Then someone comes in with medicine, and in a few minutes the pain seems to recede.

Nisagardatta keeps looking at me, and then through an interpreter asks why I have come. I say, *"For your darshan."* Silence. He asks why again. I explain that I wanted to take an interview from one of his followers, but am now on my way to Delhi. He says, *"Jean Dunn will give the interview."* She isn't present. I begin to understand why I couldn't get out of Bombay: I will have to stay for this interview.

We disperse down the staircase, and a man speaks to me, offers me lodging for the night. I am so moved—here I am once again being looked after by a stranger. By the time we reach his apartment, I learn he is the cousin of my landlord in Rajpur where I lived for six years. And not only that—he is the chief engineer of Western Railways and can get me a reservation on any train to Delhi!

We talk late into the night about the life of the spirit; he wants to hear about my travels, about the gurus I have met. Here is a wonderful example of a devotee living in the world, carrying out his worldly duties, but with his inner attention fixed. I have met many such people in India who devote their spare time to developing the inner life.

In the morning I am taken to Nisagardatta's minute house, where a gathering is again taking place, this time with Jean Dunn present. Nisagardatta seems to be much better—so much so that he attacks me harshly. "Why are you writing this book?" I explain. "Do you think," he snarls, "that you will succeed where others have failed?" It's not in my hands, I tell him. He makes dramatic, hostile movements with his arms; he yells; the disciples laugh. He insists I ask questions. I keep silence. He is infuriated. More yelling: "Get rid of all concepts! Say something!"

I keep silence. Even more yelling. I am extremely uncomfortable. I say, trying to smile, "I suppose it's better to be shouted at by an enlightened person than to be ignored by him." He gives a quarter-smile, waves his hand, and we all bow and struggle down the stairs.

I am trying to disappear as quickly as possible, too tired to cope with Sufi-Zen situations. But Jean Dunn is behind me, and to my total bewilderment, says, "We'll go round the corner—I know a quiet restaurant where we can do the interview." (She must be joking!) "No, no, he wants us to do it—it's only his way."

There's nothing to do but unpack the little black case I've been clinging to since yesterday, and turn on the tape recorder.

I am just a normal person of fifty-nine who has been searching all her life until, ten years ago, she heard of Ramana Maharshi. She visited his ashram, went back to the States, then returned to India, where she has been living for the past four years. Two years ago she met Nisagardatta Maharaj, and he became her guru.

Did he give you some form of initiation?
He gave me a mantra and initiation.

How did you first hear about him?
At Ramana Maharshi's ashram many people come to see him—there seems to be a tie.

Is it because of the similarity of self-inquiry?
It's no longer that. Maharaj has had cancer of the throat for the past year, so his teachings have been polished; he is saying he's no

longer the consciousness, he *observes* the consciousness—he's the Absolute. His teachings are now on that line.

Can you tell me something about his book, I Am That?

It's in the form of questions and answers. The fifth edition is just coming out. It came out in two volumes in 1973, having been collected and edited by Maurice Frydman, who in late life became a disciple of Maharaj. There has been no further book published. Last year I asked Maharaj—I had been recording all his question and answer periods—if he wanted me to put them together for a book. He said yes. So *Seeds of Consciousness* will come out this year. Another volume will appear later: *Beyond Consciousness.*

In spite of his illness he gives darshan *every day?*

He is in much pain at times but manages to talk twice a day. He is one of the hidden saints, so he only draws a few people at a time. His teachings aren't for the general public—we are blessed to listen to him.

How does he usually teach?

Up until his illness, it was by questions and answers. Now he will no longer teach the ABCs—he doesn't have the physical strength— he tells us the position, then it's up to us.

He seemed to insist that I ask questions.

He wants questions to come out, then there will be silence so that remaining questions will be answered within yourself.

His following is mainly Western by what I saw.

Westerners are in predominance—thousands have seen him; some for a few days, some stay months. Some he makes leave at once. He says he doesn't know why he sends people away although they want to stay.

Are you living in India on a permanent basis?

Yes, I have a residency permit. I have finished work on the second book: the work is complete. Everything he has to say has been said.

Do you ever miss Western society, your home life?

Never.

Can you say something about your personal relationship to your guru?

There are no words to describe that. . . .

Do you have an aim in life? For instance, to become one with him?
My aim in life is to lose an aim in life—that's his teaching: there's no purpose to this life; it's just entertainment. That's all.

That sounds rather Krishnamurthi-esque.
Many of Krishnamurthi's followers come here—ten came recently.

How did Maharaj attain enlightenment?
You will find that in the first part of *I Am That*. I can tell you this: the first time he met his guru—his friend insisted on taking him; he even had to buy the garland to present to the guru—he never wanted to go.

Was he very young then?
He was in his thirties. The *bidi* [Indian cigarette] shop at the corner belongs to him; his son runs it. He had eight shops, but when his guru died, he left everything, his family and business. He wandered for months all over India, until he met a fellow disciple who convinced him it was better to live in the world. He returned to Bombay, but all the shops had gone except this one. He didn't want anything; all worldly ambition had gone. When people started coming to him, he built that upstairs room.

It's minute. What are the dimensions?
Oh, about nine by twelve. I've seen that room crowded, mostly by Westerners. He says Indians are not ready for his teachings.

Do you think it was because he didn't want personal publicity that he appeared to be annoyed with me?
That's correct. I feel sure that was the idea. He doesn't want disciples—if they come, it's fine; if not, that's also fine. He gains nothing. He has reached the peak because he isn't enamored of anything the world can offer.

Does he ever talk about other gurus and their methods?
He talks about the self-styled gurus who propagate their own concepts; but there's nothing wrong with that at that level.

Does he admire any living teachers?
As far as I know, J. Krishnamurthi. In the past, Ramana Maharshi. The other day he said, "Krishnamurthi, Ramana and myself are one."

Does he advocate a vegetarian diet?

That pertains to the body; he doesn't teach anything to do with that. All he wants you to do is find out who you are.

His followers can drink and indulge in free relationships?

Whatever comes naturally to each person he should do.

He gives no ethical guidance?

No. As long as you think you are a person and this world is real, then you live by certain rules. Once you understand the complete thing, your life lives itself. . . . There are no rules, no good, no bad—I should do this, I shouldn't do that. If you think about it, all this is taking place in this life span, in this span of consciousness, and when this consciousness goes, what difference does it make?

Does he not advise detachment from worldly activities?

This comes naturally. The main and only thing he teaches is to find out who you are. The closer you come to this, the more detached you become from the world; that will happen naturally. You can't do anything to make that happen. This idea of doing something is an ego idea: "I" can accomplish. Maharaj says the consciousness drags you there by the ear because it wants to know about itself, your true nature.

What has he said about leaving the body at physical death?

For him, it will be a great festival—he's looking forward to it. For those thinking they *are* the body, it will be a traumatic experience. For an enlightened person, it's a joyous time.

When he gives you meditation, does he ask what you see inside?

There has to be somebody to see something! [laughter] . . . No, he doesn't. Visions and experiences take place in consciousness; they have no meaning whatsoever. Before you were born, did you know anything about this world? When you die—will you know anything about this world? You didn't know you existed—you exist as the Absolute, but you aren't aware of your existence. When this consciousness comes, spontaneously, you know "I am." You grab a body and become identified with that. He wants you to go back, back, away from this into your true nature. Right now it's consciousness; the longer we abide in that consciousness only and observe it, we see that everything we see is not ours—there's a "you" seeing this.

But what does he teach about God?
Without me, there's no God.

Really?
Yes.

And he's teaching that?
Yes. Was there a God before you were? Without you is there a God?

What brought me back into this body?
Do you remember a previous body?

Many people have that recollection. Are you saying we have never taken birth before?
There's no "we"; there's no entity; there's universal consciousness, which is continually expressing itself through these bodies.

Maharaj doesn't believe in karma and reincarnation?
Correct.

Ramana Maharshi taught that, surely?
They will talk to you on this level if this is your level. But if you understand what I'm saying—there's only universal consciousness expressing itself; there's no individual—then he will bring you there. He will no longer speak of this. If you die with concepts, these concepts take another form, but they will not be you—you don't know what that form will be. Concepts will come again until they are all gone.

What does Maharaj teach about selfless service, helping others?
On their level, it's good. But his teaching is that there are no others, no individual entities; everything happens spontaneously; there's no doer. He teaches: Let this life live itself and understand you are not this.

We are not "this"—then—we are "that." What is "that"?
"That" is consciousness right now.

Right now? What will it be when we leave the body?
The Absolute.

Then what comes back?
Consciousness is continually renewing itself. You throw a piece of food into a corner; within a few days, worms will come—life, con-

sciousness. The same consciousness in that worm is in you. It's not "my" consciousness, "your" consciousness; it's one universal consciousness, and that universal consciousness is you.

At our level of understanding, aren't all these concepts? Didn't you find these theories confusing at first?

The first day I came to Maharaj, he said, "My beingness is a product of food . . . and the same consciousness in the donkey was in Sri Krishna." I went to get a reservation back home; none was available, so as something inside knew this was true, I went back. He had jerked the rug from under my feet, and he kept on doing this until I lost any place to put my feet. He forces you to let go of all concepts.

Does he often send people away who come to see him?

Often. He never knows why, though. Every moment watching him is like a spectacular movie; every person's need is taken care of— I've watched that happen. You can sit quietly, but questions you have inside will be answered. Everything happens according to your need. There's no him; he has no purpose of his own: that's why this can happen. There's no ego there to bump against.

Living so close to an enlightened being can't be easy.

It's not easy if you have any ego left.

Can you say something about the positive side?

There are no words for it; everything is taken care of automatically. There's no "you" to thank God for anything anymore. You let go of everything. There's no you, no separate entity; everything is happening spontaneously. It's like there's a quiet space where you are, yet everything is happening around you.

What work did you do in America?

I worked on newspapers.

Is there a reason why people get involved with imperfect teachers?

We as human beings think there's a reason for everything; there are no reasons, no causes—it's a causeless happening. As long as we are on this human level and think there's a cause, we will be able to come up with one. If some people are taken for a ride by false gurus, you can say this is happening to them to get rid of something— whatever happens is perfect. We are just to understand there's no personal consciousness; everything is impersonal, you see.

But when we meet a perfect teacher, it's our consciousness which recognizes that, surely?
Yes.

Then our lives change.
Yes.

That's the new life?
Correct.

That's part of the divine plan requiring no effort?
No effort.

To round off, could you say what are the benefits gained from coming into contact with your guru.
I've gotten rid of the idea there's somebody going to benefit from something. . . . [much laughter]

.   .   .

I am on the night train to Delhi, still trying to work out what is happening. I know there's a purpose behind everything that's going on, in spite of what Nisagardatta expounds. After all, before I went to see Nisagardatta I was stranded; and now, not only do I have a one-of-a-kind interview, I also have, courtesy of my new friend the railroad engineer, a berth in an air-conditioned train compartment. I lie down gratefully. My guru's hand has been guiding and protecting me, giving me strength.

After a few lazy days in Delhi, I travel on to Hardwar. Anandamayi Ma is in her Kankhal ashram, and I am able to take the photographs I had missed on my earlier visit. From Kankhal, I go back to Rishikesh to photograph Bill Eilers, and he asks his guru, Swami Chidananda, to appear in the picture with him. Swamiji is telling a high official from the Delhi Department of Education about the need to give children inner education. "The outer one is all right, but how can children develop," he asks, "if the other, equally important side is neglected?" Swamiji turns to me as we go up to the roof for the photograph and says, "You should please put this in your book also."

I am back in Dehra Dun—very near my own house—trying to find out if the Sakya Lama is in residence; I still have no interviews from a Western Buddhist. Then I meet Raymond Steiner from Mussoorie, who is actually on his way to His Holiness at the Tibetan settlement in Puruwala, not far from Dehra Dun. He offers me a lift in his jeep, saying, "This is the perfect time to arrive; the teachings being given by His Holiness are almost over, and if you don't mind staying in a tent, I can help you with some interviews."

The tent is fine. And I am able to photograph the Sakya Lama with Raymond and his wife, Maree. It has been raining heavily, but Raymond, Maree and I are cuddled round the recorder. I want to know what they have been doing out here in the wheat fields, living in tents for the last three months.

*I*t appears to be one of those ironies—a fortuitous one in this case—that I've had to come all the way to this village in the Dehra Dun valley to get to know you, when we are actual neighbors in Mussoorie. Anyway, can we start by hearing about the teachings the Sakya Lama is giving here?

MAREE: They are the great Lam Dre teachings; the last time they were given in India was one thousand years ago. His Holiness has spent years preparing for this event. Monks have collected here from all over India, Sikkim, Nepal, Bhutan, Mustang, even Tibet.

Did he expect so many?

MAREE: He expected about eight hundred, and about eight hundred arrived. This new monastery was built to accommodate eight hundred. With the opening of this temple, Puruwala will now be the seat of His Holiness.

When was this Tibetan settlement started?

RAYMOND: In 1967. The teachings going on now followed the con-
secration of the monastery in December [1980].

And you have been here since December?

MAREE: Yes, and we shall now stay till the end.

How long have you been followers of the Sakya Lama?

RAYMOND: Maree has had the longest involvement—her first
meeting with His Holiness is remarkable, so you should hear that.

MAREE: Can I go back a little? We came to India searching for
something, as we wanted to leave the West. Shortly after we arrived,
we went to Bodhgaya and had a strong connection with Tibetans and
Tibetan Buddhism. We visited the Dalai Lama in Dharamsala. That
was in 1972. Then we went back to Australia—I am Australian by
birth but English by upbringing—but in 1975, I came back alone.

It was the first time I had traveled alone, and a lone woman traveling
in India is an incredible experience. Anyway, I was in Delhi in May,
hot, sticky, in a typical Hindustani situation: waiting for money to
come through. Someone wanted me to share a taxi to Mussoorie; I
accepted to escape the heat. I traveled with an American lady who
had been a Buddhist nun for seventeen years.

This lady is now based in New York and was coming back to see
His Holiness after several years. For the whole journey, she told me
about her life as a nun and all about His Holiness. As soon as I met
him, there was nothing more to say because I knew instantly I had
met the person I had come to India to meet. I had been all over India
and checked all sorts of scenes, but nothing clicked anywhere. So it
is true; when the moment is right, you meet the guru.

I had spent only minutes with His Holiness, but I had to return
to Delhi to sit it out waiting for the *paisa* to arrive. Then this girl
arrives, saying, "I don't know what I am doing here, but His Holiness
has sent me down to Delhi although I have come all the way from
New York to be with him." Then she said, "I want to invite you to
come with me to Ladakh with His Holiness's party." I wanted so
much to go, but no money; then next day—*paisa* arrived!

We flew to Srinagar and caught up with His Holiness—we were
the only Westerners. We traveled together to Ladakh. It was the first
time His Holiness had been able to visit the ancient Sakya monastery.
Ladakh had only recently been opened. I spent a blissed-out ten

days. As we arrived, there was a clear blue sky—yet it was raining.
The lamas came out dancing to receive His Holiness; it was magical.
I had my birthday there, and it was then I took Refuge with His
Holiness. I turned around and flew back to Australia and Raymond,
who was looking after the children.

When did Raymond meet His Holiness?

RAYMOND: It took a year to unstick ourselves—we had a decent
business going in Australia—but when we arrived in Mussoorie,
His Holiness had left on a world tour and didn't get back until
about two years later, in February, 1979. So I had to wait a long
time to meet him.

*But you're American by birth; can you say something about your
background?*

RAYMOND: Born in New Orleans in a Jewish middle-class family;
lived in London, where I was into films and where I met Maree.
Packed everything in so that we could get away to Ibiza, where we
opened the first vegetarian restaurant in Spain—this was in the late
sixties, probably just after you left? Then we packed *that* in to come
to India. We just flipped a coin in Barcelona to see if we should go
via the Pacific or Atlantic—crazy. We went all round through Asia;
as it came out we were to go via the Pacific.

Maree, what were you doing in London?

MAREE: I was working as a fashion coordinator—a stylist—with
photographers, for commercials, and film directors. This was from
1964 to 1968, when I met Raymond. I traveled all over Europe and
North Africa—it was fun in a way, as I was about the only free lance
stylist in London. But when I met Raymond, we both knew we had
to leave London. I didn't want Dean, our son, to have the conventional
council-school education. That took us to Ibiza.

But what made Raymond give up his film career?

RAYMOND: Yes . . . it was after the last line in a documentary we
were making on a Harold Robbins story. The director said, "It has
taken three years and twelve million dollars to bring this picture to
the screen, and I can't say I have made all the right decisions, but I
certainly have *enjoyed* it." Then he flipped a large ash from his cigar
and rode off into the sunset on a horse.

Well, I thought I didn't want to be part of spending twelve million dollars on such minus entertainment any longer; so Maree and I rode off into the sunset! I bought a still camera and since then I work with that. Hope, our eldest daughter, was born in Spain—but before she was one year old, we were off to India.

So it wasn't until the spring of 1979 that you could renew your contact with His Holiness the Sakya Lama?

MAREE: That's right. And from that time, he began preparing for these great teachings.

I seem to remember hearing that he came to visit you in your Mussoorie house.

MAREE: It was a bit strange, really, because I had gone to Bombay, but he told Raymond he would come for a visit. Naturally, [Raymond] thought it might be with a small private party, but—well, this is Raymond's story. . . .

RAYMOND: I looked out on our lawn to see about a thousand people had arrived, waiting to greet His Holiness. When he arrived, I began to understand that he was going to grant what is called Long Life initiation.

How long did this initiation go on?

RAYMOND: The place was full from 7:00 in the morning till 1:00 in the afternoon, but the actual initiation lasted forty-five minutes. Somehow we managed to put up loudspeakers. No one had thought to explain anything.

Was that when you were able to interview His Holiness? I read it quite recently.

RAYMOND: Yes, he was so co-operative and patient.

And full of humility; he referred to himself as an ordinary lama and spoke so highly of his teachers.

MAREE: They are both here. Chogay Rinpoche has come from Lumbini to be here, and Dezhung Rinpoche has come from New York to India for the first time in twenty-three years.

Can you tell me more about his relationship to His Holiness?

MAREE: He [Dezhung Rinpoche] is one of the greatest Sakya lamas. He is in his late seventies, and since he's been in America, he has recited *Om mani padme hum* one hundred million times. His Holiness has a special regard for him and considers him as a great lama with real knowledge. In making predictions, he doesn't use external objects.

I had heard so much about him; when he arrived in Puruwala I was overwhelmed—because he can't climb stairs, yet the first thing he did when he got out of the car was to try walking up the stairs to greet His Holiness. I can tell you, tears were streaming down my face—seeing this venerable lama being helped on both sides as he went up. I grabbed hold of the children and ran round the back stairs; I was able to see His Holiness come out and greet him. He was in the room where the photographs were taken. Here was his old guru back again after so many years!

RAYMOND: Incredible things have been happening. There were hailstorms threatening to ruin the wheat crop. A heavy-duty ritual master appeared, waving incense and smoke, ringing bells, and chanting, doing *puja*; the overcast sky parted and in ten minutes, there was a blue sky. And just look what happened when we arrived here in the rain; a photo call had been made so that all the lamas, monks, and lay people could be photographed with His Holiness. Two previous calls had to be canceled because of the rain, and here it was raining again for the third time. This time, some lama was asked to do something about it; it didn't actually turn into a brilliantly sunny day, but the rain stopped and the photos were taken, as you saw.

You spoke about predictions. His Holiness makes predictions?

MAREE: People are always coming, asking about this and that. The greatest lamas know what is happening; they give the answer. Others give advice through casting dice or counting beads on a rosary. His Holiness invokes a certain deity and requests an answer; he throws a dice which is influenced by the deity. Whatever the number is indicates what's to be done. The requests range from the banal to whether or not to perform surgery, or as to the whereabouts of recently born *tulkus*.

Were predictions made when the Chinese entered Tibet in 1959?

MAREE: Long before the trouble started in Lhasa, predictions indicated what was about to happen. Because of this, His Holiness was able to leave unharmed. The day after he escaped, the great Sakya monastery was entered by the Chinese; had he been there, he would never have been allowed to leave. Earlier the same year—at the age of fourteen—he had acceded to the throne and was therefore the head of the Sakyapa sect.

Why is the Sakya line hereditary?

RAYMOND: Because it's a special race—the Khon lineage; it came down directly from the Rupadhatu heavenly realm. His Holiness is the forty-first in an unbroken line of lamas that stretches back to the eleventh century.

Can you summarize the teachings you have received here?

MAREE: They have been rather intensive. We spend most of the day in the temple, where His Holiness teaches in Tibetan, sometimes up to eight hours. It's important to attend, even though we can't understand; after each session, we receive translations with the help of a Western monk, Ngawang Samten.

We have been blessed to receive these rare teachings through His Holiness, and such care and help has been extended to the many foreigners. The lamas' doors are always open, so we can get guidance. The atmosphere is so warm and friendly in the midst of such high ceremony. There are so many young monks receiving the teachings; they are a joy to watch. They are serious when it comes to the teachings, but lots of fun and not at all austere outside the temple.

Tibetans are always smiling.

RAYMOND: The training is super-intensive. In Tibet, these teachings would have been given one-to-one for nine years; here we are getting everything—including the initiations—in a matter of months. For the human mind to digest one small part is difficult.

Can you say what you intend doing when you leave here?

MAREE: We have received empowerments to practice certain meditations, so it's up to us what we do. As soon as everything is over, some of us are going into retreat for a few weeks, some for three years. For a householder like myself, one practices as much as one can weave into one's daily duties of looking after a husband and four children. To keep one's vows, one *must* practice.

Are there many Sakya Centers spread all over the world?

RAYMOND: Let me see! Well—New York, Berkeley, Seattle, and Minneapolis have centers. There are three in Canada, one in England,

one in Holland, one in Germany, one in Singapore, one in East
Malaysia, and two in France.

*When we entered the presence of His Holiness to take the photo-
graphs, why did Raymond prostrate three times?*

RAYMOND: It's out of respect to the guru, but why it's done three
times is a form of obeisance to the Buddha, the *dharma*, and the
sangha—the teacher, the teachings and the community of monks.

Are your children being brought up as Buddhists?

MAREE: Our eldest daughter, Hope, who is now eleven, is really
the one who introduced us to Buddhism. When we were in Bodhgaya,
she became totally overwhelmed with the Buddha—she was only
two—and she didn't stop saying, "Buddha, Buddha, Buddha" the
whole time. We bought her a Buddha medallion. She never stopped
talking about Buddha.

RAYMOND: She became sick not long after that; she asked for a
postcard we had of a Buddha to be placed next to her bed because
it would make her well.

The children have been here all the time?

MAREE: Oh, yes. At one point I was only going to stay for three
weeks—just for the opening ceremonies and the first teachings. Then
I decided I couldn't go; there's nothing out there in the world I could
possibly want to make me walk away from these teachings. But I had
the whole family with me, which made it difficult; so I went to His
Holiness, and he just said we should all stay as long as possible. From
that point on, I knew it was right; all the children, including Tashi
—who is two years old—took all the initiations.

One day, I knew one initiation was going to last several hours, so
I took it upon myself to leave Tashi behind; as we were about to start
in the temple, the curtain parted—there was Tashi. There was no
way she was going to be left out—she was going to take the initiation!
So far, she hasn't missed anything.

*Is it your two-year-old who demanded a blessing from Dezhung
Rinpoche?*

MAREE: You have heard about that? Well, it was the day he arrived,
and everybody of course was prostrating and offering him white
scarves. Tashi for the first time also crept up, made three prostrations
and went straight up to him—and bending her head, just stood there.

Dezhung Rinpoche couldn't see her as she is so small, but she wouldn't leave; she was just waiting for him to place his hands on her head in blessing. I had to tell one of the monks to please inform Dezhung Rinpoche to give her the blessing so that she would move out of the way. He did, and then she scrambled away quite happy.

RAYMOND: You know, the light is fading quickly, so I think you ought to finish now and I will show you to the tent for the night . . .

. . .

I have spent my first night in a tent; there's something rather cozy about tent-living—I have yet a new experience to add to the growing list, having slept in many strange places on this tour. But I slept well, and in spite of the rain, was dry.

There is a Tibetan canteen, where Raymond orders banana pancakes for breakfast, and we sit watching Tibetan life go by. Tibetans are always smiling. They have a strong understanding about dharma—to them it's a living thing. Tibetans live to gain merit so that in future lives they will be raised along the road towards enlightenment. They are conscious—that's why they can smile so much.

My next interview is with an Englishwoman who is sometimes called "Anila," sometimes "Diane," and sometimes "Tenzin Palmo." She holds much fascination, especially for the Tibetan community, because she has renounced everything to become a Buddhist nun. She lives alone in a cave in a remote part of India which is inaccessible most of the year. Tent life must be dull for her.

But in spite of her years of isolation, Anila is completely open and normal with me. A divinely contented person, she says she is happy wherever she is. Anila radiates light and balance, and her severely shaven head heightens her lean beauty.

TENZIN PALMO
Sakya Monastery
Puruwala
4 March 1981

C *an you start by telling me why you are called "Anila"?*
    Ani is Tibetan for "aunt"—all Tibetan nuns are known as Ani—
"Auntie"; the *la* is only added for respect.

What made you take such a drastic step as total renunciation?
    I first came to India in March 1964. I met my lama in June. By
the end of July, I took my first vows.

So quickly? You shaved your head from that moment?
    Yes. I came to look for my lama. It was not unexpected.

Can you speak about your background?
    I was born in England—Hertfordshire—in 1943. I grew up in East
London, where my father was a shopkeeper. When I left school, I
became a librarian. I was always interested in religion. When I was
thirteen, I read the Koran, and by fifteen, I was into books on yoga

and doing *hatha* yoga. When I was eighteen, I read a book on Buddhism; it was a simple book—*The Four Noble Truths and the Right-Fold Path*—and as soon as I read it, I knew I had always been a Buddhist.

For me, theistic religions don't reach me. The idea of a personal god is something I have never had a feeling for. On the other hand, I deeply believe in the perfectibility of the being, and through meditation we can realize our true nature. But relating to an external deity had no meaning for me. So there was Buddhism, which of course is a nontheistic type of religion, with a perfect training path of morality, philosophy and meditation.

As I knew I had always been a Buddhist, I started studying Theravada Buddhism, which in those days in London was not so easy—there were only a few Buddhists there. There was no interest whatsoever in Tibetan Buddhism, but somehow or other, at that point I read about the four sects of Tibetan Buddhism: Nyingmapa, Sakyapa, Kargyutpa, and Gelugpa. And when I read the word "Kargyutpa," something inside me said, "*Oh*, I'm Kargyutpa!" And I didn't even know anything about these sects—I had never even heard of them —but I knew I was a Kargyutpa.

Are they the yellow or the red hats?

Red. There were only two Tibetan lamas in the West at that time, and they were yellow-hat Gelugpa; they lived in Holland, but they came over to England quite a lot. I got to know them. Meanwhile, I applied for a job at the School of Oriental and African Studies in London; I was accepted, so I went to work there as a librarian. The head librarian was such a nice man, and because I told him I wanted to go to India—I had made up my mind—he said I could take a course in Tibetan and the school would pay for it. There were some Bon Po lamas there, so they taught me.

Bon Po is the pre-Buddhist religion of Tibet?

Yes. I had heard that there was an English lady, Mrs. Bedi, who had married an Indian and lived in India about thirty years; she had become a Buddhist and had started a school for young lamas and *tulkus* in Dalhousie, and also a nunnery for Kargyutpa and Nyingmapa nuns. I wrote to ask if I could come and help her. She said, "Yes, please come."

So then I started saving up to go. But meanwhile, two Kargyutpa lamas turned up, so I was very happy; one was called Chogyam Trungpa; the other, Akong Rinpoche. I had such faith in Chogyam Trungpa, although he was not the traditional idea of what a lama is like. As at that time no one was interested in Tibetan Buddhism, anyone who *was* had the lamas all to themselves, more or less. So I got to know them very well.

Had they opened the monastery in Scotland at that time?

They were still studying at Oxford—this was 1962 or 1963. I forgot to mention that six months after I became a Buddhist, my mother also became a Buddhist. So any lamas and monks we met would come to our house in London, and it was very interesting and informal. Trungpa Rinpoche had just come from Freda Bedi's *tulku* school, so he encouraged me to go there. By the time I was twenty I had enough money, so I came to India and stayed at the nunnery in Dalhousie. During the day I worked as a secretary for Freda Bedi at the lamas' school—that was in March, 1964.

Then, on my twenty-first birthday—which was in June—there was a phone call, and Mrs. Bedi answered. [Then she said to me:] Well, your best birthday present has arrived at the bus station.

Now I should go back, because two weeks before, someone asked me to write a letter to Khamtul Rinpoche; and as soon as I heard that name, I said, "Who's that?" Freda Bedi told me, "He is a Kargyutpa lama and he lives in such and such a place" and then she added, "By the way, he is coming here." I immediately said, "If he is a Kargyutpa lama, I can take Refuge with him."

So he turned up on my birthday, and I was so excited that when I walked in to meet him—I had no idea of what he looked like, whether he was old or young, or even who he was—I just *knew* he was my lama. I sat down and I was so frightened I couldn't look at him; I just saw his brown shoes and the border of his robe, and I couldn't say anything. Mrs. Bedi wanted me to say something, so I asked her to tell him I wanted to take Refuge. So she explained to the lama I was already a Buddhist and so on, and he replied, "Of course, she must take Refuge."

When he said this, I looked up—and then two things happened at the same time; one was a feeling of recognition, like: So *there* you are again! It was like seeing some old friend after a long time; and at the same time, as if the innermost core of my being had suddenly taken material form in front of me and we had never really been apart—as if he had always been inside me but now was material-ized outside.

At this point would you like to explain what taking Refuge means?

It is the entry into the Buddhist Path; one takes refuge in the Buddha, the teachings of the Buddha, and in those who practice the teachings. It dates back to the time of the Buddha himself. In the earliest Buddhist *sutras*, whenever anyone made a commitment to the Buddha's path, they would take refuge in what is called "The Three Jewels": his mind is the *Buddha*—his mind and the Buddha's are the same; his speech is the *dharma*—the teachings; his body is the *sangha*—the community of monks.

I then went back to Khamtul Rinpoche's community at Kangra and took Refuge there, and one precept. At that time I asked him if I could become a nun. He said, "For the first year I will give you the first precept: the precept not to kill—you can imagine you have all the others; but although I am not giving you them, if within one year you haven't broken any and you still want to keep them, then that's all right. So I was allowed to shave my head and put on robes from that moment.

Were you allowed to stay with your lama?

I actually went back to Freda Bedi, where I met an American girl who was a disciple of the head of the Sakyapa called Sakya Trizin—at whose monastery we are right now. This girl and I decided to travel, and she wanted to come to Mussoorie, where the Sakya Lama was then living. That is how I met His Holiness. She was also the person who brought Maree Steiner, but much later. We were able to stay one month with him. At that time, he was nineteen years old and was living with his aunt. There we took the Bodhisattva vow and a number of initiations, and he also gave us some teaching and set us to practice. He was really amazing—yes—outwardly you could say he was nineteen, but actually he could have been ninety, nine hundred. I mean, he is changeless. All these years later, he is still the same. I had much faith in him, although I was not a Sakya.

In Tibetan Buddhism one can take initiations and teachings from any of the four main branches—is that right?

That's right. It is quite a common thing to do.

Where did you go from Mussoorie?

Rishikesh, where we stayed doing *hatha* yoga; then Varanasi, and from there to Thailand, where we stayed four months. From there, I came back alone to Dalhousie, where I found my lama—Khamtul Rinpoche—had moved with his community.

When you say "community," what does that mean?

There were three or four hundred lay people, and a monastery of about one hundred monks—they had got land in Dalhousie, so they decided to set themselves up there as a craft community. I lived with them as secretary to my lama and English teacher to the children. This went on for five years, so I was also able to get teachings. But then they were given land in Kangra, so they moved again, and my lama suggested this was the time for me to break away and practice. He suggested I go to Lahaul, near Spiti, which is past Kulu-Manali. It is a Buddhist valley, lying between Manali and Ladakh.

Were the teachings given to you in Tibetan?

I could read it because I had studied Tibetan in England, but at that time, my spoken Tibetan was awful. There was one incarnate lama who would give me the actual teaching in English. My lama would indicate what I should be studying. I had now plenty to practice, so I went to live for a time in a monastery in Lahaul, which was very quiet. I stayed for five years. But as I was mainly doing retreats, I felt even this was too disturbing—living in a monastery; it can be rather sociable and sometimes noisy.

I visited my lama every year, but I wanted to go somewhere absolutely alone. I had spoken about going off and living in a cave, but everyone said, "Where there are caves with water, there are people; where there are no people, there is no water." I began thinking of building a small house, but one day when I had been looking for a site up a hillside, when I came down I felt very happy and inspired and knew something was going to happen. I had prayed very hard to my lama and to the *dakinis* for them to find me something simple and quiet, and I promised that on my part I would do nothing but practice as hard as I could.

Two days later, a nun said, "Why bother building a house—it's so expensive—better go live in a cave." Then she said, "I remember an old nun talking about a cave on top of this hill that has water and trees." Then we got it together and a party of nuns and monks went with me to look, but they kept saying, "No, no, this is too far, you can't live up here," it's too this, it's too that. . . . But when we got there, we saw it was a long overhang, and some villagers eight years before had built it up with stones to house their cattle. I said, "For sure I am going to stay here!" Everyone told me I would die of cold or there would be ghosts or thieves. Anyway, we persevered and got some carpenters to make a door and window and divide it into two rooms, and then I moved in.

How long have you lived there?
Five years. It's perfect—there's a spring with very good water; in the winter, I melt the snow—from November until May, I am snowed-in and nobody can come and I cannot leave.

How do you manage for food?
I get supplies in for one year and get donkeys to carry them up.

You can't have any fresh vegetables or fruit?
I have a little garden, so in summer I grow turnips and marigolds. The turnips are good, as I can eat the green tops and I dry them also.

How high up is it?
About 12,000 feet.

Is it incredibly cold in the winter?
Caves are warm, and I have a local square metal stove which I use for cooking and heating both. On my side of the hill, because it faces south, there are a lot of juniper trees, so I can get enough wood cut for the winter. When the sun shines, it is actually quite warm.

Does anyone come to visit you?
In the winter, no one can and I can't go down—not that I have any need, but I couldn't if I wanted to. In the summer, if I'm not in retreat, then people sometimes come from the monastery—that is the nearest place, about an hour and a half away. They come up in the spring to see if I am all right. No one can come up to find me unless there is someone to show the way. There are no paths.

So you really are cut off. How do you get your mail?
In the nearest village post office—which is three hours away— they save my mail and I collect it in May, after the snows. It's no problem. They are used to it up there. Lahaul is cut off from the rest

of India for six months of the year. Like now—I can't go back until July, as it is snowbound.

You are all alone in your inaccessible retreat for months on end— how do you pass your time?

It depends on what I'm doing; if I am in retreat, the day is divided into four meditation periods, so then I will get up at 4:00, do a session till 7:00. Then I make tea and *tsampa*, which is roasted barley flour. At 8:00, I will start another session till 11:00, which is followed by lunch: rice or fermented buckwheat pancakes, or *chapatis*, then dal and potatoes, maybe turnips. After that, I usually read Tibetan books or I copy some texts or I may paint Buddhas or bodhisattvas to give to people.

At 3:00 I have a cup of tea—I don't eat after lunch—then start another session which takes me to 6:00 or 7:00. Then I have more tea and start my evening session, which goes on till I go to sleep.

Have you ever been snowbound and unable to get out of your cave?

One year there was a freak blizzard which lasted seven days, and I was completely buried under tons of snow. It was so black and silent inside my cave, but I couldn't get out and I didn't know what to do. I decided I was going to suffocate—I convinced myself I was taking longer and deeper breaths. And although one part of me knew the air was still pure, the other was convinced I was going to die of oxygen starvation.

After six days under the snow, I was preparing to die; it was very good, because I faced up to the fact. I thought of all the bad I had ever done and felt great regret. Then I tried to think of all the positive things that had happened. But above all, I felt incredible devotion for my lama—when it all comes down to it, the only thing is the lama; that is the only thing that is going to help you. I prayed to him to bless me in the *bardo* state.

And then the thought came: Try tunneling out! Now I had a spade, and the door opened inside, so when I opened it, there was a big wall of ice. I just shoveled all the snow inside and made a small hole—it was really weird, as it seemed like going through some birth and death experience. I was in total darkness.

But after a while—about an hour—it became transparent, and gradually I got out. Only to find that everything was leveled, deep in snow: no trees to be seen, my prayer flag buried, and the blizzard still blowing. I just scrambled back inside and waited another three days till I was able to really get out.

Your practices are sacred to you, but can you say something about them?
I'd rather not. . . . I did explain that before we began.

Well, can you say why you have come down from your 12,000-foot dwelling to the plains and are living in this tent?
When I first came to India (as I explained), I spent one month with His Holiness the Sakya Lama. The following year, I was able to spend more time with him, but this time with my mother, who had come out to spend one year with me. I haven't seen too much of His Holiness since then, but nonetheless, we kept on corresponding. Last year I got a letter from him saying he was going to give his Lam Dre teaching—that is "The Path and Its Result"—and that I should attend it. For that reason alone I have come down. My lama encouraged me and said it would be good for me to come.

Can you give a description of this Lam Dre teaching?
Basically, it is the whole of the Buddhist Path, from the beginning of the renunciation of *samsara*—the round of birth and death—leading up to the fullest enlightenment, based on the Havajra Tantra—a meditation deity sacred to the Sakyas. It is a course of training started in India in the ninth or tenth century and carried over to Tibet by the early founders of the Sakya tradition; it is now only taught by them.

It must be unusually rare to have the chance to receive this teaching.
Even in Tibet, it was difficult to obtain. In India, His Holiness has given part of the teaching only twice, but here he is giving the inner teaching for the first time in India, and it is the first time he is giving the Havajra Tantra initiation to so many people. This inner teaching lasts three months because the initiations that form part of it can only be given to twenty-five people at one time. And some initiations last two days. There has also been the authoritative reading of the text connected with the Lam Dre teaching. The teaching is being given in Tibetan, but His Holiness has designated two of his highest lamas to give the teaching to all the foreigners in English. So every day

after His Holiness has finished, we gather and get it again in English. At times we feel a bit overwhelmed and overstuffed, but they have been so kind to us.

Did many disciples from abroad come specially for this Lam Dre?
Initially eighty came from Malaysia and Singapore, and they were in fact the main patrons. For example, they offered to pay for all the food so that many monks from all over India could be fed—there were about eight hundred—otherwise, for a three-month event like this they would not have been able to come here. Then about thirty-five came from the West; most of them from the Sakya Centers in the States and Canada.

Are there any other Western nuns living in India who have adopted the austere life you are following?
For many years, Freda Bedi and myself were the only Western nuns I knew of. But now there are quite a lot of Western monks and nuns, especially within the Gelugpa sect, which stresses monasticism. Some know perfect Tibetan and have spent much time studying and meditating.

For those going back to the West, it is more difficult. People there are not particularly sympathetic—society is not directed toward renunciation. In the West, just being a monk or nun raises hostility in people. Of course, if we were in lay clothes it would be all right, I suppose. Here in the East, one is freer—you can be as austere as you wish.

I don't meet so many nuns, as I am cut off. I heard recently that Trungpa Rinpoche is starting a monastery in America. There are one or two in the West already.

Having renounced the world so totally, are you ever criticized for being an escapist and turning your back on the problems of the world?
When you are living with no external distractions, then that is the time you have to face so many things: the human condition, the mind, one's nature. Then there's no escape. Yes, people in the West think this sort of life I have taken to is escapism, but one can't escape. Those caught up in Western life and its many so-called attractions are escaping. As soon as there is anything that is uncomfortable or disturbing, they have a drink, or turn on the T.V., or go to see a friend, or just smoke a cigarette—anything but turn inside and look

at where the trouble is coming from. All their senses are stimulated from the outside, everything is coming from the outside, and when it breaks down—they become neurotic.

There is this terrible fear in the West of being put into any sort of isolation—it is actually a form of punishment there; they think if you are alone for any length of time you'll go crazy. It's because they have no foundation, no idea how to look inside and learn from oneself. And they do everything in the world to avoid the one thing that is nearest to them—coming to terms with the mind.

Do you follow the Tibetan way and eat meat?

When I was with my lama I did, but now I am vegetarian; one cannot live with the idea of compassion for all sentient beings and also eat the dead bodies of animals. I do not eat eggs now. I asked His Holiness Sakya Trizin about this; he said it was a sin. This doesn't stop Tibetans . . . but I should tell you the lamas for sure—and most of the monks—do a special *mantra* before taking meat, which is intended to help whatever animal they are about to consume. In the case of the high lamas, I'm sure this benefits the animals, as there's a karmic connection.

Am I right in thinking Tibetan Buddhists don't recognize a Divine power which in the West is known as "God"?

It's like this: the highest that can be imagined is a state to be realized and not to be propitiated. What we in the West regard as the Creation is due to the power of our own deluded mind and has grown up from the beginning of time through our perverted perceptions and karma, and is held together by that. We should purify this and attain to pure vision; the external world as we see it is a perverted vision projected from our own minds.

Do you recognize such a thing as "soul"?

In Buddhism, the idea of such an innate entity—something static, permanent and always there—was repudiated by Lord Buddha. He explained it as being a mental stream, a continual changing, of coming into being and passing away. This, in its inherent nature, is emptiness—it seems to be solid to us, rather like a river. You look at a river, come back the next day; it looks the same but every drop has changed.

It seems to us we are an entity which we label as an "I," but when we search for the "I," it cannot be found. And if you turn back the searchlight on the seeker, the seeker also cannot be found; it's transparent. This transparency in itself isn't *nothing*, it's awareness, it's luminosity. At a lower level, it's compassion and love. It's not a thing that separates me from you and everything out there; in its inherent nature, it is emptiness.

How were we created?

The Buddha said there's no way to find the beginning. His mind was so extended that he could see back through eons and eons of time, through evolutions and devolutions of whole universes, but he still couldn't find the beginning. So to look for the beginning and an end is a perverted conception.

There are predictions about the imminent end of the world. What do Buddhists think about that?

In Buddhist cosmology, the universe goes into expansion and then it turns into itself—that's called the "void," the empty eon. Then again, on account of the karma of beings, the universe comes together again. So, yes, the world can come to an end, but according to Buddhist predictions, not just yet. It is, however, in for troubled times.

What do you see for your own personal future?

If left to myself, there's nothing I want to do other than what I'm doing, because I'm happy, and there's nothing else I want to do. But I do feel the time left in India is drawing to a close. If I ever left, it wouldn't be due to internal causes; it would be for external reasons. I would rather stay. . . . I feel I'm helping more beings in what I'm doing here than if I were outside doing something else. But I do feel within the next few years I will have to leave.

But wherever you are, you will go on with your practices.

I certainly hope so. Even as a child in Europe, I felt I was in the wrong place; I wanted to go to the East. I remember working out my itinerary. By the time I got to be a teenager, it was like an incredible homesickness, a pain in my heart when I heard of others going East. It became unbearable. When I had enough money to come here, everyone said, "You won't like it; you won't find anything there you can't find in your own country." The moment I got here I knew this is where I am meant to be, especially when I got to the mountains among the Tibetans. I was completely at home and I never felt homesick even for one second.

You have never been back?

Eight years ago I went to see my mother—but only for a few months.

Now that Tibet is opening up, do you have any desire to go there?

Not desperately. Anywhere I go is because there is some great lama or it is a place of pilgrimage—I don't want to go anywhere as a tourist. And in Tibet, most of the great lamas were either killed or they left. The majority of the monasteries are destroyed, so I think it would make me sad to go there.

. . .

Raymond Steiner has not only been the instrument of bringing me to Puruwala, but he is now going to take me all the way up to my home in Mussoorie. There I find the snow peaks veiled in purdah. I am happy to be at the end of this strange pilgrimage-sadhana.

But still, there is one last interview. And this one has something of a personal interest for me. Kate Christie, my wife, is a writer who has published several novels, and a book on ESP. For the last ten years, we have lived mostly in the hills away from publicity, away from our former worldly interests.

KATE CHRISTIE
Landour
Mussoorie
7 March 1981

I was born in England into a very loving family. One of my earliest memories—I suppose I must have been two or three years old—was of *someone* inside my body using the hands, walking on the feet and looking out through the eyes. During a period of illness at one point—I was ten years old—I was given a certain drug by the doctors to which one person in a thousand is allergic: I was the thousandth person. It acted on my system as a poison and I went through the death process. Death took place on three different levels. On the physical level the physical body fought like hell to live—it had everything to lose. On the mental level I was perfectly calm—and very much annoyed: I am too young to die. I have not had a chance to grow up, to develop into anybody. It's *not fair*! But there was yet another level in the very depth of me which was utterly unaffected by death.

You were aware that there was another dimension to your being?

That was what I was aware of then. Now I feel that we should surely live our lives so that this level, instead of being latent, is fully activated into consciousness enabling us to transcend physical death. Whether this death experience opened me up to certain areas of consciousness or whether I inherited the faculty of clairvoyance from my mother I don't know, but as I grew up my psychic awareness increased. I was tormented by foreknowledge of death and disaster and then forced to suffer the death—anguish of those killed in war, accident or by natural calamity. I actually saw those disembodied entities who clung to me sometimes for weeks at a time. Later it was explained to me that these entities came to me because I was a "sensitive," that's to say one of the few living persons with whom they could make contact—some of them did not know they were dead. Sometimes I knew who they were, sometimes I didn't. In desperation I tried to get help.

Couldn't you get advice from anyone?

Two things did help me: The first was the books of Carl Jung, to whom I shall be everlastingly grateful; the second was the realization that as I could get no help from other people I should have to dig understanding out of myself. Because I was a writer I decided to use the technique of writing for auto-analysis—a painful process involving the unbearable probe of *who am I*?

You were not then aware of the Indian mystic teaching of self-inquiry?

No. But I discovered that the deeper you dig the more everything breaks up under your hand. In the course of writing this book, which I called *Apparitions*, I discovered that far from being the victim of my horrifying experiences I was in fact attracting them! I myself was responsible for them. The book did help me to objectify and understand my predicament to a certain extent, and I had many interesting and even enlightening letters from readers with similar experiences. But no one can stand still; I had to move on in one direction or another. Two courses were plainly open to me: that of becoming a medium and that of learning to harness and use occult forces. In both of these directions people were waiting and willing to help me. But I had implacable blocks. To be a medium means to open oneself to God-knows-what-or-whom while in a state of trance—the dangers are obvious. And the occultist uses his powers for what purpose? To have power over natural forces and over other people. He achieves this by an aggrandizement of the will. But the mystic does just the opposite; he submits his will to that of God. So I started looking for the third door, the door of the mystic. But who would open it for me?

Then one winter when I was living in Rome I met someone who suggested meditation, and taught me what she called a Zen technique. One was simply to sit and look at a blank wall and think of nothing. I found I could leave the body very easily. But, once out of the body, all kinds of figures and situations are to be met with, and I quickly realized my friend was not competent to guide or help me. One evening I left the body in this way and found I couldn't get back. At that moment such a cry for help went up that I believe it was heard by Sant Kirpal Singh, for within a year I had heard about him and he had accepted me as a future initiate.

You are the only person in this book to have come to the spiritual path by way of psychic experiences. Have you come across any others?
Oh, yes. When I was at my Master's feet I met several. But once under the protection of a spiritual Master no occult or astral forces can touch you. And the Master would not allow us to dwell on those past experiences. The sort of meditation I was doing in Rome was taking me out through the heart chakra which is very easy—but the Master makes us go out through the third eye which is exceedingly difficult because first the mind has to be stilled. Many people coming to him from other sorts of meditation at which they'd become proficient had to start again from the beginning like babies! I refer to Sant Kirpal Singh in the past tense because he left the physical body in August 1974.

I can't ask you how you came to the feet of the Master as if I didn't know, for we are husband and wife and we came to him together. But I will ask you to describe it.
We had the blessing of coming to him at the same time, but we came from quite different angles. I have already described my crying need for a Master if I was to make any headway spiritually. In your case you'd had three careers, as a musician, as a writer and lastly as a designer. All three had been successful, but you used to say none of them gave you the deep satisfaction you needed. When we moved

from Rome to the island of Malta you had reached a point at 40 at which it did not seem worth while starting yet another career, and indeed I remember your saying it did not even seem worth while living. I think you were at the lowest ebb it's possible to reach and still be alive. Your health was gone and your spirit broken. We didn't even know why we went to Malta—it wasn't our scene. We'd lived for many years in the Mediterranean but always with writers and artists; now we were moving in among the gin-drinking retired colonels. All we wanted was some peace, so we found an old farm house we could renovate.

Unknown to us on that tiny island was one initiate of our future Master: his name was Leon Gurney Parrot. At that time he was writing to the Master that he could find no one in Malta who was remotely interested in spirituality and should he not leave and go somewhere where he could serve the Master better? The Master replied: Stay where you are; souls will be sent to you in Malta. At that time, while the Master was foreseeing our contact with Leon, I began seeing the Master clairvoyantly. He appeared as a shining figure of such spiritual power that I thought he must be Christ—the face and features were too bright to see clearly: I wondered what Christ was doing standing before me day after day—I was in no special anguish nor had I been praying to him. Afterwards I realized who it had been.

At our first meeting with Leon—when he described his own meeting with the Master in Bombay years before, and as he went on to tell of the teachings, it was as if the Master came straight through him. We both left that house with no doubt in either of our minds but that the Master had found us. It was a time of tremendous happiness. During this euphoria I thought that since I was able to leave the body I could take flight and find him. So I sat in what I called meditation and almost at once was in his presence. I saw him very clearly and very far off, like looking down the wrong end of a telescope.

He was sitting outside, as I saw green leaves behind him: he was wearing his white turban and, since it was winter, his black coat over his white cotton salvar suit. As I approached he put out his hand and said: "Don't do this. Wait!" I realized he meant me to wait for initiation, when I would have his full protection. I obeyed him. Then after a time I thought I'd just try sitting in meditation—and I found he'd blocked it! I could no longer leave the body. I thought: "Here indeed is a true Master! He is protecting me even before I am initiated." Life had taken on a new dimension. We read the Master's books and frequently met Leon.

The Master then said we should sit together in meditation. Everytime we sat, tears poured out of my eyes. And then I began to hear the Sound Current. The Master teaches that the inner Sound and Light are the primal manifestations of God, and that at initiation the third eye will be opened to see that Light and the inner ear opened to hear that Sound. The Sound comes into all religions but is called by different names; in the Bible it is of, course, the Word, through which creation came into being and by which it is sustained. Far from having to be in the Master's physical presence for initiation, aspirants not in India could apply for initiation and then sit in meditation after instructions had been read to them by whoever the Master appointed to do it—the Master Power is not bound by time and space. Indeed when we sat for initiation in Malta both of us had the inner experiences he promised. And within six weeks we had been allowed, with Leon, to go and visit him in India.

So many things happen when you are close to your Master that it's impossible to recount them all. The first thing I asked him was need I suffer the psychic phenomena which had been dogging my steps? He said no. And since then, although I am still sensitive on that level, the experiences are rare.

All during that visit we experienced many things both inwardly and outwardly, but it wasn't until the last evening that he opened the floodgates of love and poured it through us—the seal on our relationship with him, the cord with which we are forever bound to him. He told me, "I am your Father, I have you by the hand, and I shall never let you go."

That was in the autumn of 1969. We didn't see Sant Kirpal Singh again until he came on tour in the West in 1972; we were with him in London, and later joined him for part of his American tour. The tour ended in Rome and there we asked him if we might visit him in India. He said we could. Back in Malta the wish grew and grew that we might stay with him in India and work for him there. When we wrote and asked the Master, he just said he would see if we could stay or not when we arrived. At the last minute we were able to rent our house in Malta to friends from Italy; we left with one small suitcase each and have never been back. As soon as we spoke to the Master he was willing for us to stay with him and prepare some of his manuscripts for the press. In that first interview, which only lasted about 20 minutes, the majority of the literary work we did for the next six years or so had been given to us.

Living close to a Master is rather like living on top of a live volcano! As he is far more than human, his reactions cannot be predicted as they largely can in the case of a limited human being. Expecting fireworks you may get a benign pat on the head, and looking for praise you may get blame. He said himself that his angle of vision was necessarily quite different from ours. Within his radiation all perception was heightened; it was a rarefied atmosphere in which breakthroughs into God-intoxication could be followed by troughs of dark despair. Personality clashes (inevitable in any ashram) appeared to be fostered by the Master in the interests of what he called man-making. But so all-pervading was the love emanating from the Master and enveloping all his disciples that it was a whole element in which you lived and breathed, like air.

Are there any special aspects of the teachings of Sant Kirpal Singh you would like to stress?

There are two points which I think of special importance as I have not come across them expressed so clearly in other teachings. One is that the Master told us the *Attention is the outer expression of the soul.* This means that wherever we put our attention the soul will go; we can either fritter it away in outward pursuits, or we can send it inside and up on the spiritual path. He used to point out that when our attention is absolutely engaged in what we are doing we experience happiness. The other point he so clearly explained was that the sexual urge and the spiritual urge are opposite ends of the same power—he called it the *ojas* power—and you can turn it which way you like. But in sex this power is drained away. This is why everyone, in whatever religion, who wishes for enlightenment is celibate. It's not a question of repression, but simply of a new direction. Sant Kirpal Singh said that one on the Path should be celibate even within marriage, except for the procreation of children. He wanted us to be house-holders and wage-earners, not leaning on other people. He himself had married and had children and a responsible government appointment—so when we approached him we were talking to someone who could understand our problems and never spoke to us over our heads, of states we could not comprehend—he was the loving Father taking us up step by step. He said that his teaching was for everyone, and that indeed children and illiterate peasants often made better progress than people with trained and speculative minds which only stood in their way.

When we came to India our lives were completely changed. Our attention, our work, our meditation and our love were all centered on the Master.

Malcolm, now that you've traveled all over India and collected so many interviews from Westerners following so many different gurus and life-styles, I am struck by this thought: When you and I first came on the path we thought ours was the only path leading to enlightenment. We were as closed as fervent devotees so often are. Since those days a mellowing and opening process has taken place in us. I think it's because we have gradually become aware of the depth and richness of so many other spiritual paths round us here in India.

Our guru used to say: "Stay in whatever religion you already belong to—just take the next step." For us he opened the door into another dimension, that of the mystic. All mystic paths lead to the same realization. It's interesting that the teachings of some gurus are purely traditional while others vary according to the way in which each of them attained enlightenment: if it was sudden enlightenment, then the devotees are taught to work towards that; if it was through the long process of meditation or austerities, then the followers are encouraged along that path; if it was attained through self-surrender, then that will be advocated. Doubtless, Krishnamurti declared no guru is necessary because of his own life experience. But all teachers are saying, as the ancient Greeks said: "Know thy Self." They are trying to break down our self-important egos and to release the inner awareness of the true Self which is in all of us: each seeker is surely drawn to the path which is right for him.

Glossary

amrit: "nectar of immortality"; represented in certain ceremonies by a sugar solution.

arati: a devotional ceremony characterized particularly by the use of lighted candles or lamps.

asanas: term used in yoga for bodily postures assumed in meditation; the practice of *asanas* is the primary activity of *hatha* yoga.

ashram, asrama: a place of retreat and meditation; also, the term which refers to each of the four stages which make up the ideal pattern of Hindu life: *brahmacharya* (celibacy and study), *grhastha* (householding, which generally includes marriage, work, and community involvement), *vanaprastha* (retirement, or withdrawal from the world), and *sannyasa* (renunciation of worldly things and dedication to spiritual life).

aum: the three sounds composing the mantra *Om*.

avatar: an incarnation of the Divine; i.e., a person who is also fully Divine.

baba: an affectionate word for "father."

bardo: the intermediate state between death and rebirth, according to Tibetan Buddhism; it is described at length in *The Tibetan Book of the Dead,* which deals with how the soul should conduct itself in the *bardo.*

Bhagavad Gita, Bhagavat Gita, Baghavadgita: "Song of the Lord"; an important Hindu religious epic.

bhajan: devotional hymn; religious chant.

Bhakti: selfless, spiritual devotion; worship of God through personal love; *Bhakti* is one of the three most widely recognized paths of salvation, the others being *Karma* (ritual and good actions) and *Jnana* (spiritual knowledge); the *Bhakti* movement developed in medieval India and is closely associated with Vaishnava Vedanta; one who chooses this path is called a *bhakta.*

bhakti yoga: spiritual discipline which emphasizes devotional worship as a path to union with God; the "devotional" yoga.

Brahma: one of the three devotional aspects of *Brahman;* this aspect is associated with creation.

brahmacharyi: a practitioner of celibacy; often refers to one who lives as a spiritual student or seeker.

Brahman: Hindu term for the supreme reality; though Brahman is one and undifferentiated, there are three devotional aspects: *Brahma, Shiva,* and *Vishnu.*

Brahmin: the priestly caste of Hindus (sometimes spelled *Brahman*).

Buddha: an Awakened or Enlightened one; usually refers to Siddhartha Gautama, the founder of Buddhism, also known as Shakyamuni.

Buddhism: a system of thought based on the insights of the Gautama Buddha (sixth century B.C.); Buddhism is essentially nontheistic, and was originally based on a relatively simple and straightforward set of principles, articulated by the Buddha as the Four Noble Truths and the Eightfold Path; about 500 years after the Buddha's death, the original Buddhism—which emphasized the use of right action and contemplation in order to achieve Nirvana or surcease from being—became distinguished as Hinayana (represented today in the tradition of Theraveda Buddhism), and a "new" Buddhism—the Mahayana—was introduced, emphasizing as its goal the individual attainment of Buddhahood, and adding a new religious dimension of ritual and prayer; there are many types of Buddhism today, some closer to the "old" and some to the "new" model.

caste: a system of division within Hindu society; caste is based on heredity and occupation, and traditionally there was virtually no mobility or interchange among the castes.

chakra: literally, "wheel"; yogic term for a psychic center of the body; the yogic model of the "subtle body" includes seven such nodes of energy, each coordinating with certain physiologic organs and with certain aspects of spiritual development.

chela: a student or disciple of a guru.

deva (fem. **devi**): generally, a higher being.

darshan: literally, "view"; a transmission of spiritual experience, frequently silent; a collateral usage—particularly in the Northern tradition—refers to the event of a guru giving an "audience" to his followers, i.e., allowing himself to be viewed and experienced.

dharma: term used in both Hinduism and Buddhism (may be given as *dhamma* in Buddhist references) to mean duty, righteousness, the law, or the correct way, i.e., the principle of cosmic, social, and individual order.

dharmsala: a rest house for pilgrims, usually built near a temple; frequently used as a term for a guest house or hostel.

dhoti: a long cloth of white cotton, worn loosely tied about the legs and waist.

dyhana: meditation.

dyhana yoga: a spiritual discipline which emphasizes meditation as the means of achieving union with God; the "meditational" yoga.

Gurmukhi: the script of the Punjabi language, used in early religious writings of the Sikhs.

guru: spiritual master or teacher.

hatha yoga: a spiritual discipline that focuses on the relationship of mind and body; the "physical" yoga.

Hinduism: a comprehensive worldview, which functions as both a religious philosophy and a way of living followed by the majority of India's inhabitants; Hinduism takes many forms, varying significantly (both in theory and practice) from region to region, and among various guru-centered groups. But common to most forms of Hinduism is the goal of liberation from the cycle of reincarnation; there are a great many religious texts associated with Hinduism, the most widely influential ones being the Rig Veda, the Upanishads, and the Bhagavad Gita.

japa mala: "japa" meaning repetition, as of a mantra, and "mala" meaning a sort of rosary.

jnana yoga: a spiritual discipline leading to union with God through transcendent knowledge; the "mental" yoga.

karma: a term used in both Hinduism and Buddhism (may be given as *kamma* in Buddhist references) meaning "action," referring to the law of cause and effect; often used to describe the relationship between causes in a previous life and effects experienced in a present life.

karma yoga: a spiritual discipline that focuses on selfless activity and/or performance of ritual as the path to union with God; the "active" yoga.

kirtan: a group devotional event, expressed in ecstatic singing and dancing.

Krishna: an incarnation of Vishnu representing the embodiment of love; Krishna is a prominent figure in several Indian religious epics, and his love for Radha is a central theme in Indian erotic mysticism.

kundalini: a term used in esoteric yoga for an energy (also called the "serpent power" or "serpent fire") which lies dormant at the base of the spine until it is awakened through yogic practices and ascends through the body by moving along the path of the chakras.

lama: Tibetan term for a spiritual leader.

mahamantra: the "great" mantra.

maharaj: "lord"; a term of respect which may be used by or with regard to holy men.

mahatma: "great soul"; a person who has conquered the ego and achieved union with the Divine.

mantra: a term used in both Buddhism and Hinduism to refer to a word, phrase, or syllable which has sacred significance; many use a mantra in meditation.

maya: a word used in both Buddhism and Hinduism to denote the illusory nature of physical reality, or more specifically, the appearance of the One as a multiplicity of phenomena.

moksha: "liberation"; usually used to refer to release from the cycle of incarnation in the physical world.

om: the most sacred of all sounds, which contains all sounds and represents the Divine.

om mani padme hum: "Hail to the Jewel in the Lotus"; a powerful and widely used mantra.

param: "supreme."

prashad, prasad: food offered to a deity or saint; once the food has been offered, it may be consumed by the devotee.

puja: ceremonial worship of a deity.

pundit, pandit: a learned man.

raja yoga: an advanced form of mental yoga.

reincarnation: doctrine of the "transmigration of souls" from one bodily life to another.

rinpoche: Tibetan Buddhist teacher and guide.

rishi: sage or wise man; seer.

sadhana: spiritual discipline; a person following a spiritual discipline is called a *sadhaka*.

sadhu: holy man.

samadhi: the state of experiencing pure consciousness; this is the supreme goal of yoga.

samsara: the cycle of rebirth.

sannyas: renunciation of the world.

sannyasi: one who has undertaken *sannyas*, and entered the fourth stage of life (see "ashram").

Sanskrit: ancient language in which many Hindu and Buddhist religious texts are written.

Sant: "holy"; this term is used in two ways: (1) to describe a religious tradition of Northern India which is devotional, and concentrates on inner experience rather than on exterior forms, and (2) as a title applied to teachers in this tradition; it is also a popular synonym for *sadhu*.

sat: "true."

satguru, Sat Guru: a term used in the Sant tradition to refer to the inner voice of God, as mystically apprehended and experienced by the devout; the term is used by different groups and in different contexts, sometimes referring to a personal teacher who is a human vehicle for the inner voice.

satsang: a gathering for the purpose of sharing testimony of spiritual experience.

sattvic: having the quality of "goodness"; "goodness" (*sattva*) is one of the three modalities of the experienced universe, the others being *rajas* (passion) and *tamas* (darkness); the three qualities constantly interact to produce the complexity of the world.

seva: generally, "service"; either of a practical nature (in maintaining the premises and affairs of a religious site, movement, or personage) or of a broader humanitarian nature.

Shakti, Sakti: the feminine consort of Shiva; also used as a common noun to denote "energy" or "force"; when used generically ("a *shakti*") the word refers to the feminine component of a spiritual dyad; Shakti is most often worshiped as *Kali*, and *Kali*, in turn, has many forms which represent different aspects of the goddess and have different names, e.g., Durga, Parvati.

Shiva, Siva: one of the three devotional aspects of Brahman, associated with time and fertility; the masculine component of the dyad Shiva-Shakti.

siddhis: special powers (such as levitation) achieved through the practice of mystical yoga.

Sikh: the term may be used in two ways: (1) a practitioner of Sikhism, and (2) one who comes from a Sikh family and maintains the Sikh culture, but has ceased to practice the religion; there is a prescribed form of appearance for Sikh males (they typically do not cut their beards or hair and frequently wear the turban) which gives special coherence to their group.

Sikhism: a religious movement separate from Hinduism (although it retains elements of Hinduism); Sikhism is part of the Sant tradition of Northern India; it was established by the fifteenth century Guru Nanak and perpetuated by his successors, the last of whom died in the eighteenth century. Sikhism includes aspects of both Hinduism and Islam, and its tenets include the belief in one God who does not take human form, but exists as the principle of truth; the sacred text of Sikhism is the Granth Sahib.

Sri, sree, shree, shri: a title of respect, meaning generally "revered one."

Sufism: a mystical form of Islam.

Sutras: in Buddhism, scriptural works; in Hinduism, aphorisms concerning religious belief or practice.

Swami: a spiritual leader; a more specific usage refers to a Hindu initiate of a religious order.

Theosophical Society: a group formed in 1875 to promote the study of psychic phenomena and comparative religion; it was centered on the visions and writings of its founder Mme. Blavatsky and her follower C.W. Leadbeater, which brought together esoteric doctrines from many sources; though its influence declined by the 1930s, the T.S. aroused interest in Eastern spiritual traditions in the West, and is still a well-known organization, headquartered in India.

Tibetan Buddhism: Buddhism—primarily in its *Vajrayana* form—was taken into Tibet from India, beginning in the seventh century C.E.; by the thirteenth century, Buddhism had almost disappeared from India, and Tibet had begun to develop its own distinctive form of the religion, much of which is set forth in texts known as the Tantras; Tibetan Buddhism has a very rich and complex system of symbolism and ritual practice, which includes not only extremely esoteric matters, but much ceremonial pageantry as well; before the virtual destruction of Tibetan religion by the Chinese after 1958, Tibetan Buddhism (sometimes called

"Lamaism") had achieved an extensively developed network of monasteries, which served as the centers of Tibetan cultural life.

tulku: term used in Tibetan Buddhism to refer to a reincarnated lama.

Vaishnava: literally, "relating to Vishnu"; frequently refers to a particular
interpretation of Vedanta which stresses the importance of devotional
worship and the role of divine grace.

Vajrayana: the third "way" (or "vehicle") of Buddhism—a continuation of
the Mahayana tradition; Vajrayana (which is also known as *Tantric Buddhism*) places great emphasis on the use of mantras and other techniques
to enhance psychic experience, as well as on the mastery of occult
powers; the practice of this way requires initiation, instruction and
"empowerment" by a guru.

Veda: a collection of sacred texts (the Hymns, Brahmanas, Aranyakas, and
Upanishads) which are accepted in Hinduism as divine revelations; the
earliest portions of the Veda are generally thought to have been composed around 1500 B.C.

Vedanta: the most influential tradition of Hindu theology, derived primarily
from the Upanishads, and elaborating in various ways the doctrine of
Brahman.

Vishnu: one of the three devotional aspects of Brahman, associated with
existence and duration; usually worshiped through his avatars, Krishna
and Rama.

yoga: a system of spiritual discipline (associated with both Hinduism and
Buddhism) intended to lead toward union with the divine; there are
four main paths of yoga (see *bhakti yoga, hatha yoga, karma yoga,
dhyana yoga*), as well as many particular yogic systems developed by
specific sects or individual gurus; when the term "yoga" is used non-
specifically, it often refers to some form of *dhyana* yoga.

yogi, yogin (Fem. **yogini**): one who practices yoga.